W9-AEM-652

# BANANAS
## YOU CAN GROW

James W. Waddick and Glenn M. Stokes

**TROPICAL PLANTS YOU CAN GROW**: VOL. 1

STOKES TROPICALS PUBLISHING CO.

Published by
**STOKES TROPICALS PUBLISHING CO.**
Publisher Glenn M. Stokes
Published New Iberia, Louisiana USA    September 2000
Tel: 337/365-6998  Fax: 337/365-6991
e-mail: info@stokestropicals.com

First published 2000

**BANANAS YOU CAN GROW**
by James W. Waddick and Glenn M. Stokes

Series concept–James W. Waddick
Designer–Maradee Cryer
Series–Editor James W. Waddick
Photography–Glenn M. Stokes unless noted
Advisers:Tony Avent, Fred Berry, Ian Cooke, and Randy Ploetz
Text edited by Andrea Blair

ISBN 0-9678540-1-6
Printed in Ontario, Canada

Key to the bananas on the front cover:

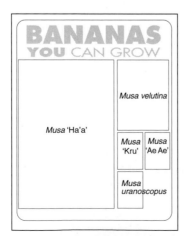

# TABLE OF CONTENTS

## ADVANCE READERS' COMMENTS

"*Bananas You Can Grow* is a long awaited and well needed resource, compiling everything you always wanted to know about growing and selecting bananas for home. Organized in an easily useable format and written in a delightful tone, tropical plant enthusiasts are sure to find this one of the most used books on the shelf."

—**TONY AVENT**, August, 2000. Raleigh, N.C.
Owner, Plant Delights Nursery

"Jim Waddick and Glenn Stokes have written the best book ever published on bananas. The color photographs of the fruit, plants, and foliage range from very good to outstanding. Stokes has traveled to most places where bananas are grown and he grows and sells banana plants and seeds in his nursery, which accounts for the wealth of photos and information.

It is amazing what you can do with bananas that so many of us didn't know, but Waddick and Stokes tell us *how to identify, how to grow, how to find*, and even *how to cook them*. For all lovers of bananas, this book is a must."

—**FRED BERRY**, August, 2000. Charleston, S.C.
Author of *Heliconia: An Identification Guide* by Berry & Kress, 1991

"*Bananas You Can Grow* has instant appeal from the many excellent and varied plates that show not only ornamental banana plants, but commercial production, fruits and tasty dishes produced from bananas. Many of the pages are flagged with fascinating "Factoids" or "Quickviews"; little snippets of easily digested information for those perusing the book rather than reading deeply.

Although this book has been written with the USA gardener in mind, I am sure that it will also appeal to the growing number of exoticists in the UK, who are successfully growing an increasingly wide range of tender plants."

—**IAN COOKE,** July, 2000. England
Author of *The Plantfinder Guide to Tender Perennials*

"As a fellow banana enthusiast, I am pleased to see the publication of this book. It represents a truly comprehensive treatment on growing, using and appreciating edible and ornamental plants in the Musaceae, and is a welcome addition to the literature on this important and interesting group. In the book, the authors cover diverse topics in a pleasing and easy-to-read format and include information on common and uncommon members of the family. Clearly, the book will be useful to the casual and rabid enthusiast alike. I recommend *Bananas You Can Grow* to all who are interested in these attractive residents of the tropical world.

—**DR. RANDY PLOETZ**, August, 2000. Homestead, FL.
Professor, University of Florida

## ACKNOWLEDGMENTS

This book is due in part to a host of people who have made suggestions and shared their experiences. Thanks to Glenn Stokes for his support of all the ideas here. David Constantine has also been more helpful than he probably realizes.

This book has not been created in a vacuum, so thanks to the "clean air" provided by the support of Powell Gardens, Kansas City friends, and especially Marty Ross. Thanks to all of them.

And to my "top bananas" who keep me from "slipping" up: Caitlin and Jim.

—James W. Waddick

I wish to acknowledge all the tropical plant experts who have fed my unquenchable thirst for knowledge about tropicals, particularly my interest in the Zingiberales, of which Musaceae is such an important group. The writing and production of this first volume of a tropical plant series has been a labor of love.

I also thank my wife, Yvonne, for her patience and understanding and putting up with my tropical plant explorations. I do want to thank my coauthor Jim Waddick for his effervescent personality and wealth of horticultural knowledge.

—Glenn M. Stokes

# Part I

# INTRODUCTION

*What you need to know about this book.*

*Musa* 'Namwah'

*Musa* 'Ae Ae'

*Musa* 'Rajapuri'

Fried plantain chips

Antique print of tropical plants (coconut, pineapple, and banana) that were obviously not seen in their habitat by the artist.

# INTRODUCTION

This is a book for anyone who wants to grow bananas. You'll find information about landscaping in tropical climates, summer bedding in temperate climates, and growing in containers, too. This is a book for gardeners. You'll find sections on cultivation, propagation, year-round care, and related practical information. We want this book to be informative, practical, and factual.

There is also a photo gallery of more than 60 different kinds of bananas in which you can compare each variety and select those that are best suited for a variety of placements and uses.

The word "banana" refers to both the well-known fruit and the plant that bears this fruit, the banana plant. Although everyone knows the fruit, few people have experience growing the plant. The plants are suitable for all climates, given appropriate care. They have large, exotic tropical leaves and can grow from a few feet tall to nearly 40 ft. (12 m), depending on variety. The fruits are delicious ripe from the tree or can be shipped great distances; some varieties must be cooked before being eaten. Other varieties are strictly ornamental.

There is increasing interest in using bananas and other large foliage plants in the landscape as well as using plants in seasonal summer beds in temperate gardens. These plants are prized for their ornamental qualities and make attractive displays as focal specimens.

This is the first book written specifically for gardeners on how to grow bananas of all kinds. It is based on years of research and first-hand experience in growing bananas in different climates and circumstances.

Bananas range in size from a few feet tall (*Musa acuminata* 'Super Dwarf Cavendish' pictured on right) to nearly 40 ft. (*Musa textilis* pictured above).

*Musa acuminata* 'Super Dwarf Cavendish' used in a landscape to create a tropical effect.

# HOW TO USE THIS BOOK

This book is composed of four major sections:

• This first section, the "Introduction."

• The next section, "Bananas in the Garden," is the main text. It contains specific information related to growing bananas. The "FAQs" (Frequently Asked Questions) cover basic questions for the beginner. Words marked with an asterisk (*) are defined in the Glossary in the last part of the book. Only their first occurrence is marked.

• The third and largest section is the "Gallery of Bananas." There are four subsections starting with the family. The second subsection consists of the three genera in the family. The third subsection is for the species – wild forms of banana still found in various parts of the world. The fourth and final subsection consists of cultivated varieties (cultivars*). These have been selected for improved fruit quality, ornamental features, or other characteristics.

• The fourth section is "Essential Information".

"Quick Views" are given for genera, species and cultivars that are widely available in commerce. These 'Quick Views' summarize information as follows:

Names: Genus—The scientific name of the three genera as currently accepted by botanists.

Names: Species—The scientific name of each species is based on the best available current information. Following the scientific name is the common name. Some alternate names may be given.

Names: Cultivars—The first name in the "Quick View" is the cultivar name that we think is most appropriate. Some bananas have been grown in many different parts of the world and have been given a number of different local names, common names and cultivar names. These names can be very confusing. We have added some of the more common synonyms following our preferred cultivar name.

Names: General – Every banana cultivar belongs to a species or is a hybrid. Where the species is known it is given such as *Musa acuminata* 'Lacatan'. Hybrids involve *Musa acuminata* x *Musa balbisiana*. These are combined in a variety of ways and the exact contribution of each species is important to commercial production. We have treated all of these simply as *Musa* hybrids. This is discussed in some detail on page 15.

Type: There are three main types based on edibility and use. "D" stands for dessert bananas; these are the common sweet bananas and can be eaten raw. "P" is for both Plantain* and other cooking bananas; these must be cooked, usually still green, before being eaten. Some of these cultivars can be allowed to ripen fully and then may be sweet enough to be eaten raw. "S" stands for species or seeded; these are generally inedible bananas used for ornamental or horticultural purposes only.

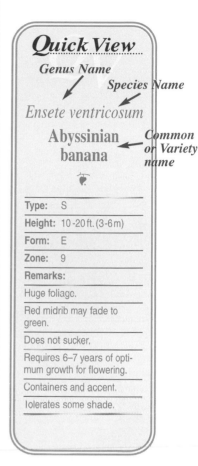

**Quick View**

*Genus Name*

*Species Name*

*Ensete ventricosum*

**Abyssinian banana** — *Common or Variety name*

| Type: | S |
|---|---|
| Height: | 10-20 ft. (3-6 m) |
| Form: | E |
| Zone: | 9 |
| Remarks: | |

Huge foliage.

Red midrib may fade to green.

Does not sucker.

Requires 6–7 years of optimum growth for flowering.

Containers and accent.

Tolerates some shade.

Bananas come in many sizes and shapes. This *Musa* 'Thousand Fingers' has a large bunch and very small fruits.

Bananas and other tropical fruits on display in an open market in Bangkok, Thailand.

Height: This is the maximum height a banana can achieve when grown under satisfactory conditions in the ground. Height is given in feet (and meters). Bananas grown in containers, harsh climates, or under other limiting conditions may reach only half this height. Height is measured from the ground to the plant's crown—not the leaf tips.

Form: "E" refers to the *Ensete* form. These bananas have a short, thick trunk with a large upright- or outward-spreading crown of leaves. "M" refers to the typical *Musa* form. These have a taller trunk and horizontal or pendant foliage. Height may range from a few feet to large, treelike heights.

Zone: This refers to USDA Hardiness Zones*. This refers to the coldest USDA Zone that is recommended for growing this banana, but all will succeed in warmer zones. Please refer to the USDA Hardiness Zone map in the Appendix. Some cultivars are not widely grown, and exact cold hardiness is still unclear. Most bananas will only flower and fruit in the warmer parts of Zone 9 and warmer. In cooler areas, mulch, cover and other protection can extend the growing range, but do not expect fruit on a regular basis. The hardiest bananas can be grown outdoors as far north as Zones 5 and 6, but are grown as herbaceous perennials and not for edible fruit. See Part 2 (Cold Climate Gardens) and Glossary for discussion of banana hardiness.

Remarks: These cover a range of special features, including: unique structures; wind, shade, or cold tolerance; ornamental features; vigor, etc. Please refer to the Appendix for related information in various lists.

• The fourth and final section is a compilation of lists, recommendations, a glossary, recipes, readings, plant sources, and related information. The detailed index allows a quick cross reference.

*Part II*

# BANANAS IN THE GARDEN

*Everything you always wanted to know about growing bananas, but didn't know enough to ask.*

*Musa* 'Dwarf Kalapua'

*Musa* 'Rose'

*Musa* 'Rajapuri'

A batik print of a banana plant.

# BANANAS IN THE GARDEN

**Petioles**

**Trunk**
*(Pseudostem)*

**Sucker**
*(Side shoot)*

**Bloom Stalk**
*(Inflorescence)*   **Fruit**

**Bracts**

**B**ananas do not grow on trees. Although many banana plants are "tree-sized," they are actually herbaceous perennials. This means they are not woody plants, but may live for years. Each banana "tree" produces a single main "trunk," known as a pseudostem*, which is made of tightly bound leaf stems (petioles*) that can reach several feet in height. Although the pseudostem may reach tree-like heights, it is never woody and rarely survives more than a few years.

Each plant produces a complex bloom stalk (or inflorescence) that produces the fruit we know so well. The banana stalk blooms just once in its life, then it dies; it will not produce another stalk of fruit. Most bananas produce side shoots known as suckers, and as the "mother plant" matures its fruits, these suckers will grow and in turn flower and fruit, continuing the cycle of the original planting or mat*. When a sucker is detached from a "mother plant" it becomes a separate banana plant. Some bananas can only be grown from seed as they do not produce suckers readily.

## THE FAMILY

The banana family (Musaceae) is native to Southeast Asia and surrounding tropical and subtropical regions, Africa, and Madagascar. The family is composed of only three genera*. The first genus*, *Ensete*, contains a small number of species and is now found in Africa, Madagascar, northern India, and western China. The most important species is *Ensete ventricosum*. By far the largest and most important genus is *Musa*, which contains most of the edible bananas and most of the ornamental species. This genus contains some of the most economically important plants in the world.

The third genus is *Musella* from southwestern China, with a single species, *Musella lasiocarpa*. It is highly ornamental although it does not produce edible fruit.

### RELATIVES

The banana family is closely related to seven other tropical plant families. The Strelitziaceae includes the well-known 'Bird-of-Paradise' (*Strelitzia*) and the 'Travelers Palm' (*Ravenala*), which is often mistaken for a banana. The heliconia family (Heliconiaceae) has a single genus, *Heliconia*, which consists of perhaps more than 300 species. These plants also have very banana-like

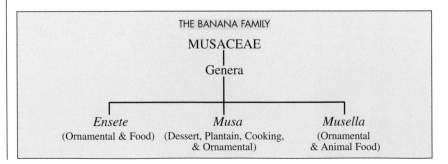

| THE BANANA FAMILY |
|:---:|
| MUSACEAE |
| Genera |

| *Ensete* | *Musa* | *Musella* |
|:---:|:---:|:---:|
| (Ornamental & Food) | (Dessert, Plantain, Cooking, & Ornamental) | (Ornamental & Animal Food) |

foliage. The canna family (Cannaceae) also has only a single genus of plants, which are grown worldwide for their bold foliage and colorful flowers. The ginger family (Zingiberaceae) and the related costus (Costaceae) family includes dozens of genera with more than 1,200 species, which are grown for spices, cut flowers, medicinal herbs, ornamental foliage, and the landscape. The prayer plant family (Marantaceae) is an important group of plants (with as many as 500 species in more than two-dozen genera) grown in the tropics for starch production, and as ornamental and as container plants because of their vividly colored foliage. The last family in this parade of relatives is the Lowiaceae, which has a single genus, *Orchidantha*, grown by a few collectors of exotic plants (see page 35).

### THREE TROPICAL PLANT FAMILIES RELATED TO THE BANANA

Heliconia family
(Heliconiaceae)

Canna family
(Cannaceae)

Ginger family
(Zingiberaceae)

## BANANA TYPES

In common terms, there are three major groups of bananas—the two that produce edible fruits, and the one whose fruits are ornamental only. Dessert bananas produce the well-known fruits that can be eaten fresh and make up the agriculturally important varieties grown for international commerce. Cooking bananas consist of two genetically different groups. The pure plantain and the cooking bananas are indistinguishable in the market. Both types produce similar fruits which have more starch and are less sweet than dessert bananas. Generally these types must be cooked (usually when still green) before being eaten. Most cooking and plantain types are grown and eaten locally. Ornamental bananas are mostly wild species that are grown for the beauty and form of their foliage, flowers, or (mostly inedible) fruits. All types of bananas will be considered here. See the discussion later in this section for details.

## PLANT

The banana plant develops from an underground bulb-like stem structure technically called a rhizome*. This is somewhat similar to the rhizomes of its close relatives, such as *Heliconia*, *Strelitzia*, and others. The rhizome has a small central growing area (the meristem*) from which the leaves develop. Each leaf is composed of a long sturdy petiole and bilateral blade. These petioles are tightly wrapped around each other to form the pseudostem (main stem) of the banana plant. Each leaf is wide with a strong central midrib*—characteristic of all bananas. The largest banana leaves can grow to 15-ft. long and 4-ft. wide(4.6m by 1.2m).

**THE THREE BANANA GENERA:**

ENSETE

MUSA

MUSELLA

As the banana plant grows, and growth will vary from one variety to another, a terminal flower bud develops. There are many factors related to flower and fruit production. See the "FAQs" (at the end of this section) for details. Technically the banana plant produces a head of flowers or an inflorescence composed of colored bracts and dozens of flowers. As this inflorescence grows it protrudes from the center of the leaves, elongates, and produces female, complete, and male flowers. The female flowers are produced first and are the ones that will produce the fruits. After flowering and fruiting, the banana plant will die, but before and during flowering, the plant produces shoots or suckers around its base, or at a short distance away, to continue its survival.

### EDIBLE BANANAS

One of the most perplexing questions about bananas is how the edible seedless fruits ever originated and how they reproduce. Bananas have been known for thousands of years, long before recorded history. The method of giving names to plants dates back to the Swedish botanist Linnaeus who described and gave us the names *Musa paradisiaca* (for the plantain) and *Musa sapientum* (for the 'Silk' or 'Apple' dessert banana ) more than 200 years ago. According to ancient tales, the banana was the tree in the Garden of Eden that bore the forbidden fruit, and the name *paradisiaca* refers to this tale of paradise. Another tale says that in India, wise men ate from a certain tree known to bestow wisdom, thus the species *sapientum*, meaning "wisdom." Time and knowledge have changed and today we know that these particular bananas are the specific cultivars 'French Plantain' and 'Silk Fig' respectively, and not species of bananas.

It is now known that almost all edible bananas, whether dessert, cooking or plantain types, are derived from the two wild species: *Musa acuminata* and *Musa balbisiana*. Botanists can determine just how much of a contribution each of these species has made to modern cultivars and these cultivars can be designated by a set of handy abbreviations. *Musa acuminata* in "short-

*Musa acuminata 'Dwarf Cavendish'*

*Musa balbisiana*

hand" is AA for the diploid species, AAA for triploids and AAAA for tetraploids; similarly, plants that are derived completely from *Musa balbisiana* are indicated as BB, BBB or BBBB depending on the number of sets of chromosomes. Plants that are completely derived from *Musa acuminata* (AA, AAA or AAAA) are typically dessert bananas. Hybrids between these two species can have a variety of abbreviations including AAB (which are the typical plantains), ABB (which are also cooking bananas) (both triploids) to ABBB (a tetraploid cooking banana). Many edible bananas belong to the 'Cavendish' group which are all classed as AAA. Most botanists involved in agricultural studies use this shorthand to separate the true plantains (AAB) from cooking bananas (ABB, AAB and some AAA).

Wild species are diploid and produce hard seeds in a soft pulp. Edible bananas are generally parthenocarpic, seedless and therefore sterile. The earliest seedless varieties were propagated by suckers and divisions. Today with modern methods of micropropagation this is the predominant means of propagation.

*Musa acuminata* 'Dwarf Red'

*Musa* 'Orinoco'

*Musa* 'Pitogo'

Banana fruits come in all shapes and sizes. The smallest edible bananas may be less than 2 in. (5 cm) in length while the largest plantain can easily reach 2 ft. (.6 m) long. The outside color can be red, pale yellow to rich yellow and gold, dark green, or blue-violet. Inside the fruit can be white, cream, pale yellow, pale orange, or pink. A single plant can produce a few dozen fruit at a time or hundreds of fruits.

Banana fruits can be straight, slightly curved, or very curved; other shapes can be triangular, square, or flattened ovals. A few are even ball shaped.

Shown above are just a few of the shapes of banana fruits.

OTHER USES

Most parts of the banana plant are edible and useful. The fruits are eaten raw or cooked in many different cuisines around the world. The flavor of bananas is, of course, a matter of individual taste. Experienced tasters rate the flavors of some species to be the traditional "banana" flavor; other species are noted to have hints of the acidity of apples or pineapples; some suggest the flavors of melon, peach, or even ice cream. Plantains can vary from very tart to bland and starchy. Most plantains should not be eaten raw and unripe, but some, if left to ripen on the plant, will become sweet enough to eat like a dessert banana. Few are highly esteemed compared to true dessert bananas. In Thailand, the cultivar 'Namwah', a cooking banana is a popular baby food when it is allowed to ripen fully.

The leaves can be used as serving trays or plates for prepared foods. The leaves are also commonly used to wrap foods for storage or cooking. Food is divided into individual servings and wrapped tightly in banana leaves, then steamed or roasted. The leaves trap in moisture and tolerate the heat without imparting any flavor to the food: very handy, clean, and disposable.

The rhizomes are eaten by both humans and livestock. Some species have large, starchy rhizomes that can be dug, peeled, and stewed for human consumption, while others are simply dug, chopped, and fed to pigs, cattle, and other animals. In Ethiopia, the cooked rhizomes of *Ensete ventricosum* are an important staple food for almost eight million people. The rhizomes of *Musa basjoo* are cooked in a winter stew in parts of west central China.

The pseudostem can also be cut and chopped to feed cattle and other livestock. The immature flowers of some bananas are a common ingredient in some oriental foods.

Bananas and parts of the banana can be used to prepare an entire meal from soup and salad to main course, dessert, and drinks. See a few recipe recommendations at the end of this book.

## CULTIVATION

### PLANTING

Bananas are best planted at the start of the growing season. In warm climates, planting at the beginning of spring or the spring rains helps get them established. In cooler climates, hardy bananas also benefit from spring planting, which helps them settle in for the shorter growing season. Container bananas also benefit from this head start.

### FACTOIDS

In Costa Rica, the time from planting to harvest is as little as 7 months. In cooler subtropics, this time may be up to 16 months.

The main importers of bananas are the U.S., European Union, Japan, and Canada.

Plantains being sold from the back of a truck along a highway in Puerto Rico.

Bananas being cleaned and inspected in a packing warehouse in Martinque. Above: Cut into hands for packing. Right: Bunches being checked for insects and other "critters."

Photo by Caitlin Waddick

Bananas are best purchased as potted plants. These can be purchased any time but should be planted in a protected well-lit spot when the temperature is above 57°F (14°C). If they cannot be planted immediately, keep them from freezing and in as warm and bright a spot as possible.

Plants may be shipped from mail-order sources as potted plants with or without their pot and with or without soil. These plants are best potted in a loose soil mix as soon as possible and allowed to establish before planting in their final destination. Care should be taken that newly potted plants are not exposed to extremes in terms of high/low temperatures, strong sun, and overwatering.

Smaller-sized bananas and most ornamental varieties are excellent in containers. Be sure to allow ample space for growth and enough soil volume to give root room. A single *Musa velutina* can grow well in a 10–15 gal. nursery container (approximately 15 in. [37 cm] in diameter and height) but a larger container is even better. Bananas are heavy feeders, so at planting time a handful of a slow-release fertilizer should be mixed with the soil used in the lower half of the container. After filling the container, add a top dressing of organic mulch including some manure or fortified compost. Usually such a container will be fine for a couple of years, but the banana will need replanting and a change of soil by the third season.

### FERTILIZATION

Bananas are heavy feeders and drinkers. Best results are obtained with slow-release fertilizers at the time of planting and an organic mulch at the soil surface. Regular application of granular fertilizer at the beginning of the growing season will yield good results. Liquid fertilizers can be applied throughout the growing season according to specific instructions.

Bananas will do well with an even fertilizer such as 6-6-6 or 12-12-12, but a higher potash or potassium level, such as found in 6-2-12 or 9-3-27, results

**FACTOID**

Paper made from banana fibers is a fast-growing alternative to traditional paper pulp.

Photo by Caitlin Waddick

Left: Whole bunches of bananas being transported by cableway system to a factory in Costa Rica for processing prior to export. Above: Bananas bagged for protection from pests, diseases, and wind damage in the field before harvest.

## FACTOID

Most bananas are grown commercially between latitudes 20˚N and 20˚S of the Equator.

A diseased banana leaf.

Wind damaged leaves are unsightly. Select wind resistant varieties or grow in a sheltered location.

in better flowering and fruit production. Always be sure the fertilizer includes all the trace elements. All bananas prefer a slightly acid soil, and a few prefer an even more acid soil (pH below 6.0), so acidified fertilizers can be used a couple times a year. It is best to have your soil tested to know the exact pH of your soil.

Watering bananas can be tricky, especially indoors and in winter. If the leaves fold up, hang, or curl they may not be getting enough water; or they may be getting too much water. Brown leaf edges are also signs of water stress. Make sure the soil does not hold too much water and drains well. The most common cause of death for bananas, especially in containers, is water-logged soil. Air cannot get to the roots, and the plant suffocates.

Containers should be watered until the water drains out, then allowed to dry out long enough for the first couple of inches of soil to dry out before being watered again.

### PESTS AND DISEASES

Fortunately home growers have few problems compared to those sometimes found in large commercial plantings in the tropics. The two major fungal diseases of bananas are Panama disease and Black Sigatoka, a leaf spot disease. Some cultivars are more susceptible to these diseases than others. These diseases should not cause a problem for the average home gardener.

Insect pests range from borers to grasshoppers and are controlled by specific pesticides. Root nematodes are more difficult to control. The major problem is not noticing the damage or the plant's slow decline. The best cure for all these conditions is careful observation, isolation, and treatment. Diseases and pests are most often spread by lack of careful hygiene: moving infected plant parts and soil from one plant to another.

### OTHER PROBLEMS

Far more damaging for home gardens than pests and diseases are climatic conditions. After all, gardeners want plants to look good in their gardens. Occasional hard frosts in warm climates may kill all the foliage and make the plant look terrible; however, plants will usually recover. In cold climates fall and winter freezes will "kill" a plant to the soil level. Even a hard freeze will rarely penetrate through the pseudostem down through the soil to the rhizome.

Even more routine is the damage caused by high winds. Some bananas have delicate foliage and will shred in the lightest breeze, while others are nearly windproof even in strong winds. To ensure good-looking and unshredded foliage, select more wind-resistant varieties, usually the shorter growing varieties that can be protected by fences, hedges, walls, or overhead trees.

Bananas may be especially subject to wind damage when fruiting. The extra weight of the head of fruit can tip over the entire plant. Fruit heads may need extra support with a wood or metal tripod holding the base of the bunch and stabilizing the entire plant.

# PROPAGATION

## SUCKERS

Eventually you will want more than one banana. You can either buy a new variety to expand your growing collection, or you can separate the suckers off your own plant. *Ensete* bananas rarely or never make suckers, but other *Musa* varieties and the *Musella* can be expected to produce a number of new suckers each year. Growers classify as many as four different kinds of suckers, but the commonest are "sword suckers" bearing narrow sword-like leaves and "water suckers" which are more superficial in origin and have wide leaves. These are sometimes called "spears" or "umbrellas" which are also descriptive. The "sword suckers" are the prime sources for new plants.

In order to obtain a sucker, carefully dig down around the sucker selected for separation. Make sure the sucker already has good, healthy roots. Clear the soil back as close as possible to the main rhizome and, using a clean sharp knife, shovel, or axe, cut the sucker free of the main rhizome. Try not to break or pull off roots on the detached sucker. The sucker may be several inches tall in *Musella* or 4–5 ft. in some *Musa*. A sucker 1-ft. tall with a leaf or two is ideal. Clean the cut surface and dust with a powdered fungicide or a bit of rooting hormone with fungicide already in it. You may rest the plant in shade for as long as a day or more to allow the cut surface to dry and heal before replanting.

This new sucker is ready to plant where you wish. The success rate of this procedure is very high, and it allows you to exchange plants with fellow gardeners or expand your own plantings. Some bananas are very prolific in sucker production, and you may remove a half-dozen or more suckers at a

**FACTOIDS**

Bananas grow best at a pH of 5.8–6.5. This is a slightly acid soil.

Bananas stop growing below 57°F (14°C).

During warm season growth, bananas produce an average of 4 leaves per month.

*Musa acuminata* ssp. *zebrina*

Aerial photo of banana plantation on Costa Rica's Pacific coast, however most export production is grown on Costa Rica's Atlantic coast.

time. Do not remove all the suckers, but be sure to leave one or more good suckers to replace the "mother plant" after it has produced fruit and died.

If you cannot plant a newly separated sucker right away, wrap the root ball in damp newspaper and/or moist peat moss and keep it in a cool, dry spot for a couple of days. Well packed and protected, these wrapped plants can be sent to friends as a way of sharing your bounty. Just be sure they are free of disease and pests.

### SEEDS

Many ornamental banana species may be grown from seed. In most seeded species the fruit is composed almost entirely of large, dark seeds in a starchy pulp. Some seeds may be as big, or bigger, than a garden pea. The seeds are very hard and durable. The seeds should be cleaned of all pulp, rinsed and brushed clean. Soak seeds in warm water and a mild fungicide for 24 hours, as this can speed up germination. Seeds can be planted in pots or in the ground and covered with 1/4 in. (about 1 cm) of soil and placed in a warm (80°F; 27°C) bright site, but not in full sun. Fresh seeds can germinate as quickly as 2 weeks, but some varieties will germinate slowly over a longer period of time—more than 6 months in some, depending on condition and cultivar or species.

Once the seedling has produced its first leaf, gradually introduce it to full sun. A seedling banana can grow to 6 ft. or more in a single growing season depending on variety. These new seedlings need careful watering and almost constant fertilizing (as much as once per week) for optimal growth.

### MICROPROPAGATION

Bananas have met 21st-century technology. Using standard techniques of micropropagation, a new cultivar banana can be multiplied very quickly under sterile laboratory conditions. This is an exacting and expensive proposition, but it has already made many "new" banana cultivars available to commercial growers and home gardeners. Tissue culture* can produce thousands of genetically identical plants or clones for planting a new plantation.

The home gardener has benefited by tissue culture, too. Until recently the Chinese Yellow Banana (*Musella lasiocarpa*) was thought to be extinct. Plants were found and slowly brought into cultivation at very high prices. Just a few years ago a limited quantity was offered at more than $300 a plant. Thanks to the use of tissue culture, these plants can now be purchased for very little expense, and this formerly rare banana is now common enough to grow as a ground cover.

## GROWING BANANAS IN COLD CLIMATES

Bananas are always a focal point in a colder climate garden. Today there are more ways than ever to grow bananas, even in the far north. Bananas, and other large foliage tropical plants, have become the focus of annual display gardens in the north. A single banana is the instant center of attention in a garden. The banana plant's distinctive foliage and impressive form is a very popular complement to larger annuals. Bananas can be planted in the ground as temporary specimens or planted in containers that are moved into place for the growing season.

---

THE DAILY IBERIAN — WEDNESDAY, FEBRUARY 9, 2000

**Some flower**

A young boy takes a closer look at a golden lotus flower at the Chinese Gardens Tuesday in Singapore. Brought in from China to celebrate last weekend's Chinese New Year, the flower's appearance is exotic compared to local flora.

Pictured above is a clipping from a US newspaper showing the flower (incorrectly identified as a golden lotus in Singapore) of the Chinese Yellow banana (*Musella lasiocarpa*).

Container bananas can be placed on the patio or deck, near a pool, or anywhere their foliage will accent the landscape. Be sure to provide bright sun, but be wary of potential wind damage. Sometimes prevailing winds can whip around a corner and destroy a banana in a sudden storm.

### GREENHOUSE

The easiest way to grow bananas in cold climates is in a warm greenhouse. The warm, moist conditions in a heated greenhouse are ideal for bananas. Provided that there is enough day length, bananas will fruit regularly in places as far north as Iceland.

Greenhouses provide warm, humid, and wind-free locations for bananas where they will grow to perfection. Not only can you grow the most tender of tropical edible bananas, but ornamental sorts such as *Musa*'Ae Ae' and all the *Musa ornata* cultivars can be exceptionally lovely. They need the same care as bananas grown in the ground in mild climates. Greenhouse bananas may be grown in the ground or in large containers. Temperatures should be kept between 57°F (14°C) and 95°F (35°C).

### CONTAINERS

The most common way to grow bananas during summer in the north is to plant them in large containers placed in full sun and water and fertilize them well. Top dressed with organic fertilizers, mulches, and compost, bananas in containers will stay in peak growing condition all summer, until temperatures drop below 57°F (14°C) in the fall. Many people grow bananas in large containers; wooden boxes, large plastic tubs, or even metal wash tubs—all work well. In the fall and winter, these planters can be brought into a warm greenhouse or a home to continue the bananas' growth. The plants should not be exposed to temperatures less than 57°F (14°C) or growth will stop. They should be given bright light, but reduced water as their growth will be slowed by shorter days and duller skies.

If you wish to halt the growing process of your container bananas over the winter, withhold water gradually and place them in a cool, dimly lit garage or basement. Once the plants have acclimated to cool temperatures and reduced

Photo by Markku Häkkinen

Above: *Musa* 'Namwah' growing in Heleniski, Finland.

Left: *M. acuminata* 'Super Dwarf Cavendish' bananas on ground level of a planter at the Iberia Parish courthouse, New Iberia, Louisiana.

water, they can be exposed to lower temperatures down to the mid-30s (°F)(3°C) without experiencing permanent damage. These plants should not be allowed to grow as new growth under these conditions will be very weak. The reduction in heat, light, and water will put the bananas "on hold" until warm weather returns. Gradually the soil will dry out and the leaves will dry, wrinkle, and drop. It is possible to cut back all foliage to the top of the pseudostem producing a bare "stalk." When these plants are gradually returned to more sun, warmth, and water, new growth will appear quickly and look great. Sturdy plants like *Musa* 'Rajapuri,' *Ensete ventricosum*, and *Musa acuminata* Cavendish cultivars respond well to these treatments.

A more difficult wintering process can be attempted by bringing potted bananas into a warm room such as a sunroom and keeping them active and growing all winter. Growth will slow down because of the short days of winter. The typical dry atmosphere in modern homes will dry out the bananas, causing dry leaves or brown leaf edges. Large banana plants make difficult houseplants, but smaller plants should do well if you have a large, well-lit bathroom, which is usually the most humid room in the house. Try *Musa acuminata* 'Super Dwarf Cavendish,' Chinese Yellow Banana, or one of the smaller ornamental species. But any variety can at least potentially be used as a winter houseplant. Regular misting of the foliage (twice a day) and grow lights are recommended.

Some success is also possible using very large containers. Purchase or build a waterproof box about 3-ft. (1 m) long on each side. Drill holes in the bottom of the box for drainage and mount it on rollers or wheels before filling the box with dirt and planting a banana. Once it is filled with soil, the box will be very heavy. This large box can be rolled in and out as weather permits and can stay out all summer. Planter boxes and large pots can also be moved from indoors to out with a hand truck or dolly.

### FORCED DORMANCY

Hardy bananas can also respond to even more drastic treatments. Plant them in the ground in spring at the start of warm weather and give them optimum care all summer. After all the foliage has been "melted" by the first frost, the banana is cut back to the top of the pseudostem. This leaves a totally bare, leafless stalk. Dig up the large root ball and knock off most of the soil. Wrap the root ball in a few layers of newspaper, being careful not to damage the roots or the rhizome. Place the rhizome and 6 in. of the bare pseudostem in a large plastic garbage bag. Wrap and close this bag around the root ball and secure loosely at the top of the bag.

This will look like a large, odd baseball bat. Lay this down flat on a cool basement or garage floor kept above 45°F (9°C) and ignore it until spring. You might want to check that the root ball does not dry out completely during winter. The pseudostem should remain firm and succulent.

When the days warm up enough (57°F and warmer) the "dormant" plant can then be planted outside. Prepare a new hole with enriched soil and plant to same depth as previously grown. New roots and new leaves will appear shortly. Of course, care should be taken to not overwater or overfertilize at this time.

### HARDY BANANAS

Although this may sound like an oxymoron, some bananas are hardy enough to be grown outdoors in the ground as far north as USDA zone 5 with some care; in hardiness zones 6 and 7, these hardy species need less winter precautions.

In the farthest north zones, the gardener should plan ahead. Plant the hardiest rated species and cultivars close to the foundation of a house or heated building to absorb some residual heat and protection. Otherwise, place where the banana plant is protected by a stone or concrete wall, foundation, a large rock, etc. These rock-like structures will absorb heat, even in winter, and keep nearby soil temperatures slightly warmer than surrounding soils.

Then grow the plant as well as possible all summer: fertilizing, mulching, and watering appropriately. With the first frosts, the tender foliage will freeze, turn brown, and die. Harder frosts will eventually turn the pseudostem to "mush," too. After the pseudostem is totally frozen, cut the stalk down to within a few inches of the ground. Pile a foot or more of loose, dry leaves over the stem and a foot beyond in all directions. Straw or dry oak leaves are excellent and form lots of enclosed small air spaces as insulation. On top of this place an old blanket, sheet, or insulating garden fabric made just for this use. Anchor each corner to keep this "insulator" well tucked in all winter. You may also pile more leaves on top.

As warm weather returns, slowly remove the protective layers. Start by removing just the top layer of leaves or the protective cloth cover. Wait until the weather warms even more, then remove leaves gradually after all chance of frost has passed. Finally remove all leaves and observe the old pseudostem base, which may have turned into an icky, slimy, smelly mess. You will think all is lost, but after removing the soft or decayed parts, expose the remainder to the sun and warmth; it will soon dry, and the central meristem will start to grow and new leaves will shoot up.

If the weather has been very extreme or the protection does not match the severity of the cold, the main rhizome may freeze, but usually new shoots will appear and grow. Shoots may sprout from a few inches to a foot away from the main rhizome of the previous year.

Plants will grow as temperatures warm, and a species such as *Musa*

**FACTOID**

Bananas do not grow on trees. The plant is an herbaceous perennial closer to a lily or canna than any woody plant.

Pictured above and to the left is *Musa basjoo*, Japanese Fiber Banana, the world's most cold-hardy banana.

Bananas can make a phone booth in New Iberia, Louisiana look tropical.

*basjoo*, one of the hardiest, can get to 10 ft. by fall. Usually they will also put up multiple stems and make lots of new growth. Follow instructions for mulching, watering, and fertilizing.

For the in-between zones 6 and 7, follow similar instructions, but less protection is needed. Hardy species may overwinter without protection. They will die to the ground, but resume new growth in spring like cannas, hardy lilies, and other herbaceous perennials. Naturally one cannot expect fruiting under these difficult conditions, but a hardy species like *Musa velutina* routinely makes fruit and produces seed even in zone 7. Other smaller ornamental varieties should be tried.

The basic advice is to protect the rhizome. The more winter protection, the further north these can be grown. The more parts of the plant that are protected from freezing the better chances of success. It is possible to build a wire cage, or a wood or carboard box around a pseudostem, fill this protective box with leaves, insert a small heating coil or light bulb. All this must be monitored to provide just enough heat to keep the pseudostem from freezing, but discouraging active growth. The pseduostem may also be wrapped in layers of insulation, straw and other materials. Plants so covered may keep the pseudostem alive all winter with this protection and increase both the active growth in the following summer and increase the chance of flowering. These extra protections require some trial and error and you may experience total loss.

Of course it is best to select the plant with the most hardiness potential, site it well and give it good care when it is growing actively. Actual survival and growth will vary from one year to another, but it is very possible to grow excellent banana plants with minimal extra care in USDA Zones 5 and 6 as the senior author has done in Kansas City, MO for around ten years.

## GROWING BANANAS IN MILD CLIMATES

Bold foliage plants and brightly colored flowers are the hallmarks of tropical and subtropical gardens. Bananas, palms, gingers, and other "exotics" seem totally at home in such gardens. Bananas can be used in a variety of ways in tropical climates. Bananas grown under perfect conditions in the ground will always reach their largest size and vigor in the tropics.

### SPECIMEN

The simplest and most frequent use of bananas is as specimens, either as single plants or as clumps of bananas consisting of mature pseudostems and their suckers (termed a "mat"). Specimens may be fruiting varieties grown for home consumption or ornamental varieties grown for their landscape quality, color of foliage, flowers, or fruit.

Ornamental bananas are especially showy in tropical gardens where large clumps of flowers can be grown for their most dramatic effects. Perhaps the most effective specimens, where space allows, are any of the *Ensete* species, noted for their huge, upright leaves and distinctive form. An individual plant can reach imposing proportions in a short period. The typical green foliage of *Ensete ventricosum* or the red wine-colored foliage of *Ensete maurelii* can be an instant centerpiece to a garden area. Neither of these bananas make suckers, so the effect of a single huge plant is not diminished by competing suckers.

## LANDSCAPING

Bananas planted in the ground reach their finest potential. The plants will be taller, more robust, and most vigorous. Using cultivars that reach different sizes and forms, bananas can be worked into the landscape in many unique ways.

Bananas such as *Musa acuminata* 'Super Dwarf Cavendish' or Chinese Yellow Banana can be used as a ground cover. The former has become quite popular in coastal U.S. areas. New plants should be planted fairly closely and allowed to grow together to be a true ground cover. These smaller bananas can grow to only 2 or 3 ft. in height as a thick ground cover. Since little light actually reaches the ground, there are few weed problems when using bananas as a ground cover planting.

Because bananas naturally form clumps (except *Ensete*), they are natural substitutes for shrubs and small trees. Viewed in this manner, a medium-sized banana of any sort can be planted and allowed to form shrublike clumps in the garden. Of course bananas do not lend themselves to traditional pruning, but removal of suckers will contain plants to a specific area.

The tree-like bananas are most imposing and can form the main structure of a garden and give it an ever-changing flexibility. Because an individual pseudostem is fairly short lived and new pseudostems will grow to replace existing plants, the placement of bananas as a "tree" will not be as stable as a palm tree or other woody plant. Bananas as trees tend to "move around" in the landscape, which can be very appealing.

Landscaping with bananas whether as trees, ground cover, or specimens means variation in season, fruit, and possibly placement, as successive generations of new pseudostems come up in places slightly different from their original planting plan, thus resulting in a flexible landscape.

A specialized planting of bananas is that for fruit production.

Photo by Maradee Cryer

Pictured above is a clump of *Musella lasiocarpa*, Chinese Yellow Banana. In coastal U.S. areas, bananas such as *Musa acuminata* 'Super Dwarf Cavendish'(center photo) or Chinese Yellow Banana may become quite popular as a ground cover.

Left: A *Musa acuminata* ssp. *zebrina* is the focal point in a tropical garden in Baton Rouge, Louisiana. Surrounding the banana are Caladiums, a 'Persian Shield' (*Strobilanthes dyeranus*) and *Coleus*.

Technical books have been written on timing, spacing, and production strategies (see "Additional Readings" in the back of this book). Tropical gardeners may plant a couple of good fruiting varieties for their home consumption, but home "orchards" are less common. Home banana plantations are subject to special considerations and information should be sought in specialized publications.

### PLANT COMPANIONS

Bananas by themselves do not make a landscape or decorative planting in tropical or temperate gardens. This book is for gardeners who demand a blend of plants to produce a pleasing overall effect. Although bananas have distinctive broad foliage, their frequent tall bare stems need some companion or associate planting that will add beauty and variety to your plantings.

### CONTAINERS

In a large container the form and foliage of any banana can be truly impressive, but, especially in northern climates where fruit is unlikely, there is little to offset the solid green of the leaves. The large broad foliage forms a very useful canopy over smaller plants growing around the base of the container.

Photo by Maracee Cryer

The dark maroon underside and the spotted leaves of the Blood Banana (*Musa acuminata ssp. zebrina*) add a touch of drama to any garden.

Pictured on the right is a garden in Baton Rouge, Louisiana, featuring an *Ensete ventricosum* (Abyssinian Banana). Brightly colored caladiums and coleus are used as bold companion plants at the base of the banana.

Photo by Maradee Cryer

Any summer annual suited to bright sun or light shade will help to cover the base of the pseudostem and give color and excitement. Even the modest impatiens, marigold, petunia, and zinnia get added interest because of their contrast with the focal-point planting. It is also possible to add more excitement with plants that have both color, form or texture. For example the clambering nasturtiums will use the pseudostem as a prop and climb and lean on the pseudostem while their bright yellow, orange, or red flowers add bright spots of color.

Vigorous annual vines such as morning glories should be avoided as they can actually surround the unrolling new foliage and prevent its proper release and expansion.

Brightly colored foliage of coleus (now *Solenostemon*) are very useful for their contrasting foliage. Clumps of ornamental grasses or the fine fernlike leaves of cosmos also make elegant counterpoises to the large foliage of the banana, adding color, form, and texture.

Avoid heavy-feeding and large-growing bulbous plants and perennials as the container may be subject to temperature and water extremes that will damage or weaken all plants. Remember the banana should remain the focus of these containers, and companion plants just add interest.

### LANDSCAPE

In the tropical landscape, bananas can be used as a basic skeleton and intertwined with a host of other beauties outdoors. Some of the best are small- and medium- sized gingers both for their flowers and range of foliage. Individual gingers can function as ground covers (*Kaempferia*), shrubs (many species), or offer wildly variegated foliage (some *Alpinia* and *Zingiber* to name a few).

Try to avoid plants that look too much like bananas such as heliconia and larger Canna varieties as this does not diversify the plants as much as the spiral gingers (*Costus*) or palms.

Dense mats of bananas can provide shade so avoid plants that need higher light levels such as plumeria or hibiscus unless you can provide a brighter area or plant these varieties near the edges of large clumps.

There are many tropical plant combinations that are possible; try to emphasize bright colors, contrasting foliage shapes, sizes, and textures to diversify the plantings. Be careful that all this color and texture does not interfere with the bold statement that bananas of all kinds provide.

The *Musa acuminata* 'Super Dwarf Cavendish' banana is a good choice for a container in a small garden.

*Photo by Maradee Cryer*

The broad leaf foliage of a banana provide nice shade for *Kaempferia* gingers.

*Photo by Maradee Cryer*

Siam tulips, *Curcuma alismatifolia*, growing under a banana in Chiang Mai, Thailand.

Banana fruit will take 2–4 months of peak growing conditions and care to ripen.

## GETTING BANANAS TO FRUIT

There are many factors that need to come together for a banana plant to produce fruit. Obviously bananas fruit best in warm, tropical climates where they have an uninterrupted growing season of 9–15 months or longer depending on variety. During this growing season, the temperature cannot drop below 57°F (14°C) for any extended time. The growing plant must have just the right amount of fertilizer, water, sunshine, and care. There is considerable research that the banana plant must produce a minimum number of leaves before the flower will develop. This number will vary from about 9–12 leaves at the time of flowering.

The flowering head will develop over the course of a few weeks to a month, and then the fruit will take another 2–4 additional months of prime weather to ripen. During this time, extremes of temperature, fertilization, and watering should be avoided. High winds can easily topple a banana plant holding a large bunch of fruit. Some banana growers brace developing fruit with wood, bamboo, or metal supports.

There are only a few select spots in the tropical climates of the world where all these factors come together to make commercial banana production possible. This points out the added difficulty of producing fruit in cooler, less amiable climates.

Commercial banana production for export occurs world wide, with the greatest exporters in South and Central America. Ecuador, Costa Rica and Honduras are the major producers. Bananas are also grown and consumed locally in Africa (Ghana), Brazil, Australia, Southeast Asia (especially India) and the Caribbean. Most bananas (around 85 %) are produced and consumed locally.

Large commercial producers pick and ship bananas when fully formed, but green in color. Bananas ripen at the final market destination. Ideally all fruit arrives at its destination still green. Fruits are treated with ethylene gas to induce the final ripening process so that ripe or nearly ripe fruits appear in local markets.

Even a few marginal climates produce bananas mostly for local consumption including parts of Florida and California in the United States, and Crete, Israel, Egypt and Morocco in the Mediterranean area. Many cultivars of bananas are grown throughout less developed countries and consumed locally because export quality standards cannot be met.

A few will fruit in zone 8 (and then only in warmer microclimates), even fewer in zone 7 with lots of special care. North of zone 7 successful banana fruiting may result in a newspaper article. So although "tree-ripened" bananas may not be likely in New York City or Chicago, these are still prime areas for growing bananas for their tropical foliage and ornamental flowers, and as dramatic summer garden accents.

## THE FUTURE

While it is seldom possible to make accurate predictions, the future of bananas is very bright, mostly because of continued improvement in commercial crop production. Many new hybrids have been produced by banana research stations to improve disease resistance, flavor, wind resistance, shipping and storage qualities. Rare and little-known wild species are being rediscovered and observed in nature and are coming into cultivation with potential for producing more ornamental and hardy varieties.

One of the oddest new varieties is the 'Burmese Blue Banana'. This is a seeded (fertile) form of *Musa balbisiana* that when ripe has a skin that is bright blue-violet in color. It is edible when cooked and is highly ornamental. Wild species from higher elevations in Tibet and Himalayas, such as *Ensete glaucum* and *Musa sikkimensis*, may be hardier than other species now in cultivation. These "new" species may also contribute new genetic combinations to our edible banana hybrids.

Verging on science fiction, a number of researchers at the Boyce Thompson Institute for Plant Research at Cornell University are already testing new genetically engineered banana varieties that contain elements that, when eaten, will produce antibodies and immunities to such diseases as hepatitis, cholera, and related diarrheal maladies. Even babies fed a small portion of these bananas can produce resistance to diseases that are highly fatal in many tropical countries. The fruits can be locally grown and their administration does not require hypodermic needles, sterile conditions, medical personnel, or all the related costs. Dr. Charles Arntzen and his coworkers will soon be conducting real-world field trials.

A related research study focuses on finding and selecting banana varieties that have a higher percentage of storage protein. This study can help develop edible vaccines by providing a better delivery of the desirable materials.

NASA scientists working with indoor air quality in the space shuttle and with the development of the "Biodome" experiment, discovered that plants grown indoors could significantly improve air quality. *Musa acuminata* 'Cavendish' was selected as among the fifty best in removing volatile organic compounds from indoor air and improving its quality. Formaldehyde and other toxins were removed from the air along with a dozen or so other chemicals tested and a variety of "bioeffluents" produced by people. Plant growth also increased the presence of water vapor and suppressed spore development in these enclosed environments.

A "personal breathing zone" of 6–8 cubic ft. was especially improved by nearby plants. This is a volume comparable to a small office cubicle, or the area around a desk where a person may stay relatively static for hours on end. So it can be said that indoor plants improve local air quality. This work continues (see "How to Grow Fresh Air" in "Additional Readings" at the end of this book).

The future holds more and better bananas for consumers and gardeners, medical treatment in poor tropical countries, improved indoor air quality, and so much more.

**FACTOIDS**

*The New England Journal of Medicine* reported that a banana can cut the risk of death from strokes by as much as 40% in certain cases.

The average American consumes around 25 lbs. of bananas a year, every one of them imported from Latin America.

*Musa balbisiana* 'Burmese Blue Banana'

Photo from *Plants and People of the Golden Triangle: Ethnobotany of the Hill Tribes of Northern Thailand* with permission from Edward F. Anderson.

## FAQs—Frequently Asked Questions

**How do I get started growing bananas?** Just do it. Obtain one of the species or cultivars suggested below depending on whether you want it for a landscape element in a mild climate, as a container plant, in a greenhouse, or as a hardy perennial in your cool garden. Some mail-order nurseries offer beginner's collections, which is an ideal way to try a range of good beginners' bananas. First decide what kind of banana you want.

**If I wanted just one banana, which one would you suggest?** That depends on where you live and what you want to do with it. Two all-around good cultivars for the landscape or for containers and that winter well indoors are *Musa* 'Rajapuri' and *Musa* 'Dwarf Cavendish'; both have tasty fruit, too. *Musa basjoo* is rated as the cold hardiest. *Musa velutina* is very ornamental and is considered a "first" banana by many. These last two are ornamental and do not produce edible fruit.

**What is the best banana for growing in a container?** All bananas prefer full sun, so a banana in a container is a perfect "show-off" for any sunny patio or deck. Use a large container: at least a 15-gal. pot (15 in. [38 cm] diameter) filled with a rich well-drained soil or soilless mix. Chinese Yellow Banana (*Musella lasiocarpa*) retains a good size and form, while *Musa* 'Rajapuri' has high wind resistance. The larger the container, the larger the banana you can use. Smaller ornamental flowering bananas such a *Musa ornata*, *Musa uranoscopus*, and *Musa velutina* provide great color, too. The *Musa* 'Super Dwarf Cavendish' or *Musa mannii* stay small enough to fit in a decorative pot right on the patio table. Just remember, bananas in pots need lots of water and ample fertilizer. Flowering ground covers and annuals are great companions in big containers.

**What is the best banana for growing indoors or in the greenhouse?** Highly ornamental bananas such as those with colorful flowers (*Musa ornata*) in a range of colors, or those with variegated foliage (*Musa* 'Ae Ae' or *Musa acuminata* ssp. *zebrina*) will justify the use of house or greenhouse space. Any of the dwarf bananas are good because they take up less space. Remember, the greenhouse must be maintained above 57°F (14°C) to keep bananas actively growing and fruiting. Bananas also need very bright light, so site plants indoors near a large south-facing window or appropriate artificial light. The *Ensete* cultivars make an imposing display, but can get large.

**What is the best banana for landscaping?** In a tropical climate you want bold foliage, so try an *Ensete* or a wind-resistant variety such as *Musa* 'Rajapuri.' In a protected site, try the brightly variegated *Musa* 'Ae Ae' or the easier grown *Musa acuminata ssp. zebrina*. If there is ample space, use a tall variety such as *Musa* 'Red Iholene' or *Musa* 'Ele Ele' ('Black Hawaiian'). Bananas can act as trees, shrubs, ground covers, or specimens in warm-climate gardens.

**What is the best-tasting banana?** Everyone's tastes differ, but many people like *Musa* 'Mysore,' *Musa* 'Rajapuri,' and *Musa* 'Ice Cream.' Once you have tasted a fresh home-grown banana, you won't want store bought again. The new import *Musa* 'Kru' is also getting high marks for great taste. *Musa* FHIA-01 ('Goldfinger') is also excellent.

**What is the best cooking banana?** Cooking bananas and plantains, have special requirements, as some taste different if cooked green or ripe and depending on the recipe. The famous dish tostones is best from *Musa* 'Dwarf Puerto Rican' or *Musa* 'Huamoa,' while the *Musa* 'Saba' and *Musa* 'Giant Plantain' are rated a bit sweeter. Some bananas are great if cooked green, but also get sweet enough to eat fresh, too. This is great double use from one plant.

**What is the hardiest banana?** Hardiness is due to many factors, not just winter cold. Bananas need plenty of warm weather in their prime growing season, so if your warmest season rarely gets above 80°F (27°C), they may have less hardiness. Even so, *Musa basjoo* is usually considered the hardiest, but will lose all foliage and may die to the ground north of zone 8. *M. basjoo* has tolerated temperatures below -20°F (-29°C). North of zone 5 you'll need more mulch and protection. Limited experience with *Musella lasiocarpa* suggests it may be nearly as hardy, and *Musa velutina* survives and fruits outdoors in zone 7.

**What is the tallest banana?** Most bananas have been selected to be short enough to have accessible fruit, but there are a few giants. *Musa* 'Ele Ele' ('Black Hawaiian'), the Philippine *Musa* 'Saba,' and *Musa textilis* all get to around 25 ft. (7.5 m). They are all wind resistant, a necessity at these heights. At the 20 ft. (6 m) height, you have a larger choice, including *Musa* 'Brazilian,' *Musa* 'Giant Cavendish,' *Musa* 'Monkey Fingers,' *Musa* 'Red,' and *Musa* 'Green Red' to name a few. *Musa* 'Orinoco' is commonly seen on the streets of New Orleans and the Gulf Coast of the U.S. At 17–18 ft., it averages slightly shorter.

**What is the smallest banana?** *Musa acuminata* 'Super Dwarf Cavendish' is a mere 2–4 ft. (.6–1.3 m) tall. It is used increasingly as a ground cover in mild climates, and on occasion produces edible fruit. *Musa mannii* (from Assam, India) grows to 2–3 ft. high (.6–1 m) and has small seeded fruits.

**How do I get my banana to make fruit?** This is a complex question with many factors. Basically bananas need between a nine to fifteen month growing season (above 57°F) to produce a flower and another two to four months or more to ripen the fruit. They also need an ample number of leaves to produce flowers (9–12 leaves depending on cultivar) and at least 4–6 leaves must be present to mature fruit. They also need full sun, ample fertilization (especially high in potassium) and good watering. In cooler climates this may mean a warm winter greenhouse to encourage year round active growth.

**When is the best time of year to plant a new banana?** All bananas should be planted at the start of their growing season. In the southern U.S. (zones 8, 9, and 10), that may be as early as February and March, while in zone 6 or 7 growth doesn't begin until April or May. This gives garden-grown bananas the full growing season to get established and show off to their best right away. Bananas grow fast, so a small, 1-ft. tall plant, properly planted early in the season, may top out over 10 ft. in the first season, depending on cultivar. In the true tropics, plant them before your main growing or rainy season, but, practically speaking, bananas can be planted any time good growing conditions exist.

**What kind of soils are best for bananas?** In general bananas are not fussy and can tolerate a range of soils from sand to clay and in between. Any good soil with a loose texture is preferred. The soil should hold water, but never become water logged. They all prefer an acid soil (pH* 6.0–7.0) and few kinds (including *Musa* 'Ae Ae' and *Musa* uranoscopus, Red Flowering Thai) do better in even more acid soils (see the specific recommendations).

**When should I fertilize bananas?** Bananas need feeding constantly during the growing season. Newly planted bananas should have a handful of slow-release fertilizer in their planting hole. Once the cool season arrives, cut back on fertilizer and water. You may use organic fertilizers or chemicals, solid or liquid. You can use a balanced fertilizer such as 6-6-6, 10-10-10, or 12-12-12 for regular maintenance. For optimum flowering and fruiting, use a fertilizer higher in potassium, such as 6-2-12 or 9-3-27. Be sure the fertilizers are complete with all other minor elements. Bananas are most in need of higher potassium levels applied early after planting and again about 3 months later. Flower and fruit production is determined at about 5–9 months of age.

**Why did my banana die?** There may be many reasons. After a banana plant fruits, that plant always dies, but suckers are produced during the growing season before the "mother plant" dies. This is normal and expected. After harvesting the fruit, cut the banana pseudostem back to about 6 ft. (1.8 m). This allows the rhizome to reabsorb nutrients stored in the pseudostem. When the pseudostem falls over, cut it to ground level and dispose of it.

Some bananas are less resistant to cold and can die if exposed to extended temperatures below 57°F or to frosts. Cold-resistant bananas will bounce back quickly after cold exposure, and the hardiest bananas can take extended freezing temperatures. Too much or too little water can result in death, too. Rarely, bananas can be killed from too much fertilizer.

Pests and diseases may also prove fatal, but these are unlikely unless you live in a warm, tropical climate and these factors are present.

# Part III
# GALLERY

*Featuring "Quick View" summaries of information on each variety. Each "Quick View" consists of species and cultivar/variety names; plant type, height, and form; hardiness zone, and special-feature remarks.*

• **The Family**
*and its close relatives*

• **Genera**
*Three varieties*

• **Species**
*Wild forms of bananas*

• **Cultivars**
*Cultivated varieties of bananas*

*Ensete maurelii*

*Musa hybrid 'Iluamoa'*

*Musella lasiocarpa*

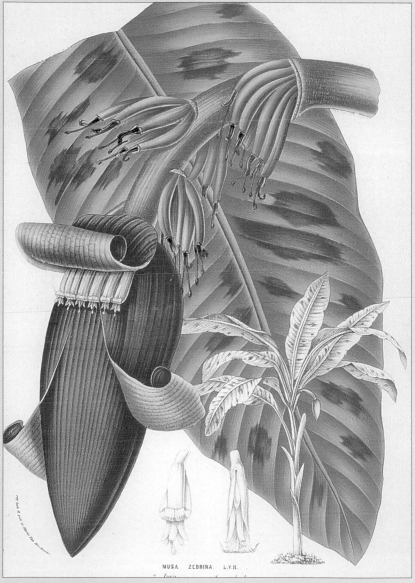

Antique print of *Musa zebrina* (from Java); now correctly known as *Musa acuminata* ssp. zebrina.

# THE FAMILY

## Quick View

## MUSACEAE

The banana family originated in the Southeast Asia and the Western Pacific where most wild species still occur. There are only three genera *Ensete*, *Musa* and *Musella* found from Australia to southern Asia across to South Africa with outposts in the Himalayas, central China and Japan. *Ensete* may have originated in Africa where most species in this genus are found. There are three types of bananas: dessert or sweet bananas, plantains and cooking bananas, and various horticultural/ornamental species and varieties. Today edible bananas of all types are grown in all countries where the climate permits.

*Musa acuminata* ssp. *zebrina*, a red and green banana grown for its foliage.

*Musa* 'Praying Hands,' a banana with unique fruit that resemble pairs of hands.

The flowers of the *Musella lasiocarpa* Chinese Yellow Banana.

Commercially grown bananas, like this *Musa* 'Mauritius', are picked green, but home gardeners can allow fruit to ripen.

Relationsips of the banana family (Musaceae) to their relatives in the Zingiberales. Diagram from *Heliconia: An Identification Guide* (Smithsonian Institution Press) by F. Berry and W. J. Kress (used by permission).

*Musa ornata* 'Hybrid Globe'    *Musa* hybrid 'Orinoco'    *Musa acuminata* 'Monkey Finger'

Example of the forms of various banana bunches; upright, pendant, widely spaced.

# RELATED PLANT FAMILIES

The banana family is closely related to seven other tropical plant families.

Strelitziaceae
Heliconiaceae
Cannaceae
Costaceae
Zingiberaceae
Marantaceae
Lowiaceae

*Canna (Pink Sunburst)*
*Cannaceae*

*Ginger (Costus barbatus)*
*Zingiberaceae*

*Heliconia psittacorum*
*Heliconiaceae*

# THE FAMILY

*Musa* hybrid 'Namwah'

*Ensete sp.* (growing on cliffs in northern Thailand)

*Musa* hybrid 'Rajapuri'

*Musa acuminata* 'Lacatan'

# THE GENERA

The banana family **(Musaceae)** is composed of only three genera.

*Ensete* contains a small number of species.

The largest and most important genus is *Musa*, which contains all the edible bananas and most of the ornamental species.

The last genus, *Musella,* has a single species that is ornamental and bears inedible fruit.

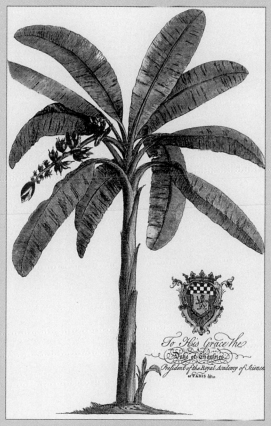

Antique print of unknown origin of a *Musa* species.

# THE GENERA

## Quick View

### ENSETE

**Species:** Around 6 or 7

**Height:** Can grow up to 20 ft. (6 m)

**Origins:** Africa, Madagascar and Southern Asia. Now worldwide.

**Hardy:** Zone 9 and warmer. Some species may prove hardier.

**Remarks:**

Does not form suckers.

In Ethiopia, cultivars have been selected for their edible rhizomes.

Seeds are very large.

All have very large, upright paddle-shaped leaves forming a crown of foliage.

Pseudostem base is usually markedly swollen.

Excellent as accents in landscapes and containers.

Upper photo shows a group of *Ensete maurelii*. Lower left photo shows the beginning infloresence of an *Ensete ventricosum* flower. The far right photo is an example of the *Ensete ventricosum*.

# THE GENERA

## Quick View
### QV
### MUSA

**Species:** Around 40

**Height:** Varies from 2 ft. (.6 m) to more than 30 ft. (9 m)

**Origins:** Southeastern Asia to Australia. Now worldwide.

**Hardy:** Varies. A few species are hardy to zone 5–6, some to zone 7–8; most are hardy in warmer climates.

**Remarks:**

Most sucker readily.

Many produce edible fruits, including sweet or dessert bananas, plantains and cooking bananas..

There are many ornamental seeded forms.

Typical banana form—upright "trunk" with pendant or erect fruits and arched foliage. Includes seeded and seed-less forms.

Good for all uses.

Upper photo shows *Musa ornata* 'Milky Way' in bloom.
Left photo is *Musa acuminata* 'Dwarf Cavendish' with fruit.
Right photo is Costa Rican *Musa* 'Creme.'

# THE GENERA

## *Quick View*

### *MUSELLA*
### Chinese Yellow Banana

🍌

**Species:** Only 1 known

**Height:** 6 ft. (1.8 m) but may get taller

**Origins:** Yunnan Province, China

**Hardy:** At least to zone 7 and warmer, but may prove hardier.

**Remarks:**

Suckers readily.

Produces small, inedible fruit with large seeds. Large yellow bracts surround small yellow and white flowers.

Excellent in landscapes and containers.

Flowers last 6-9 months.

Leaves are tough and wind resistant.

Not widely grown.

The large photo shows a mat of plants with some in flower. The closeup (right) shows the actual flowers held tightly within the bright yellow bracts.

# THE SPECIES

**Species:** The scientific name is based on the best available current information.

**Varieties:** The first name is our selected variety name. Some popular banana varieties have been grown in many parts of the world and have been given a number of different names. Names that appear in single quotes are cultivars (see Glossary). Names not in quotes are common names. Variety names can be quite confusing.

**Type:** All of the following species are listed as "S" which we have used to mean both "species" and "seeded". These are generally inedible bananas used for ornamental or horticultural purposes.

**Form:** "E" refers to the *Ensete* form. These bananas have a short, thick trunk with a large upright- or outward-spreading crown of leaves. "M" refers to the typical *Musa* form. These have a taller trunk and horizontal or pendant foliage. Height may range from a few feet to large, tree-like heights.

**Zone:** This refers to USDA Hardiness Zones. See map on page 121. Minimum hardiness zone is listed, however most will be hardy in warmer zones. Please refer to earlier comments on hardiness and expect flower and fruit production only in warmer parts of Zone 9 and warmer. In colder zones, these may be grown as ornamental and herbaceous perennials.

# THE SPECIES

## Quick View

*Ensete maurelii*

### Red Abyssinian Banana

| | |
|---|---|
| **Type:** | S |
| **Height:** | 10-15 ft. (3-4.7 m), possibly taller |
| **Form:** | E |
| **Zone:** | 9 |
| **Remarks:** | |
| Colorful foliage. | |
| Huge leaves. | |
| Does not sucker. | |
| Containers and accent. | |
| Tolerates some shade. | |

This is a huge ornamental plant with leaves up to 10 ft. (3 m) long. The deep red color of new foliage fades slightly as the plant matures, but the color is exceptional. This banana does not produce suckers so it must be grown from seed or by tissue culture. Very fast growing, but difficult to flower in northern climates. Fruits have very large hard seeds and are inedible. Makes an outstanding focal point in a large container in a display greenhouse. This species grows wild at high altitudes in eastern Africa.

# THE SPECIES

## Quick View

*Ensete ventricosum*
**Abyssinian Banana**

| | |
|---|---|
| **Type:** | S |
| **Height:** | 10-20 ft. (3-6 m) |
| **Form:** | E |
| **Zone:** | 9 |
| **Remarks:** | |
| Huge foliage. | |
| Red midrib may fade to green. | |
| Does not sucker. | |
| Requires 6–7 years of optimum growth for flowering. | |
| Containers and accent. | |
| Tolerates some shade. | |

Beginning inflorescence pictured in inset to left.

A very large plant that makes an excellent specimen in warm climates. Tolerates some shade, so does well indoors in a large space. Does not sucker, so it is grown from seeds or by tissue culture. Young plants are very fast growing and may reach 8 ft. or larger in one season. Excellent for large containers. The huge leaves (to 15 ft. [4.5 m]) often show a red midrib, but color varies and may fade as the leaf ages. It's sometimes grown as an annual for display only. This species grows wild at high altitudes in eastern Africa.

# THE SPECIES

Photos on this page by Randy Ploetz

1

2

3

4

Selections of *Musa acuminata* exhibit a range of sizes, foliage, and fruits as seen in this array of photographs.

1. 'Rose' AA is shorter form of 'Rose' pictured on page 94; this 'Rose' is used in breeding (CIRAD-FLHOR, Guadeloupe).

2. 'Pisang jari buaya' AA, common name is 'Crocodile's Teeth' in Malay; also known as 'Monkey Fingers'.

3. 'Pisang lilin' AA which is recognized as a derivative of *Musa acuminata* ssp. *malaccensis*.

4. 'Veinte cohol' AA which is a derivative of *Musa acuminata* ssp. *microcarpa*.

This is the wild species that is one of the parents of nearly all edible bananas. Wild plants are mostly seeded and inedible. Wild, seedless plants are also known and these have fruits that are sweet when ripe and usually eaten fresh. The species and its subspecies are widely distributed from Southeast Asia to Australia. *Musa acuminata* is also the parent (with *Musa balbisiana*) of most modern cooking bananas and plantains.

# THE SPECIES

## Quick View

*Musa acuminata*
ssp. *zebrina*

**Blood Banana**

**'Rojo,' 'Zebrina'**

*Musa acuminata*
var. *sumatrana*

| | |
|---|---|
| **Type:** | S |
| **Height:** | 10 ft. (3 m) |
| **Form:** | M |
| **Zone:** | 8–9 |

**Remarks:**

Multiuse banana for indoors or out. Winters well indoors in the north.

Fruit small seeded and inedible.

Dramatic foliage and form.

Containers and accent.

Recommended.

This is one of the most beautiful of all ornamental bananas. There are various slightly different forms (leaf shape, height, color) in cultivation that give rise to all its common names. The foliage is red or "wine-stained" and striped. The foliage is long and wide and shows off well in the landscape, in both containers and indoors under high light conditions. It is widely available and often grown as an annual in northern gardens.

# THE SPECIES

**Quick View**
*QV*

*Musa balbisiana*

| Type: | S |
|---|---|
| Height: | 14 -15 ft. (4.3–4.5 m) |
| Form: | M |
| Zone: | 9–10 |
| Remarks: | |

Endemic in Southeast Asia.

Relatively drought tolerant.

Fine-looking tall specimen.

Seeded

A very impressive plant that is tall and majestic. One of the original parent species of most of the present day edible bananas although it is not edible. The other parent species is *Musa acuminata*. This species in the main contributing parent of the true plantains and most other cooking bananas.

Mat of *Musa basjoo* growing in Portland, Oregon. (Photo courtesy of Burl Mostul)

# THE SPECIES

## *Quick View*

### *Musa basjoo*
### Japanese Fiber Banana

### Hardy Banana

| | |
|---|---|
| **Type:** | S |
| **Height:** | 14 ft. (4 m) and taller |
| **Form:** | M |
| **Zone:** | 5 if protected; 7 unprotected. Possibly hardier. |
| **Remarks:** | |
| The hardiest known banana. | |
| Tropical foliage. | |
| Containers and accent, | |
| Highly recommended and very versatile. | |
| Seeded. Seeds easy to sprout and grow. | |

This banana is native to the Ryukyu Islands of Japan. It is among the farthest north-growing of all bananas. Gardeners have experimented growing this as far north as USDA zones 5 and 6. This has been a proven performer in western Europe, southern Canada, and northern United States. Of course all above-ground parts freeze to ground level, but the rhizome survives and produces new pseudostems that can grow to 10 ft. or more in one season. It produces small, seeded, inedible fruit. In past times the strong fibers in the trunk were used to make fabrics. A variegated foliage form has been reported, but is not yet available in commerce.

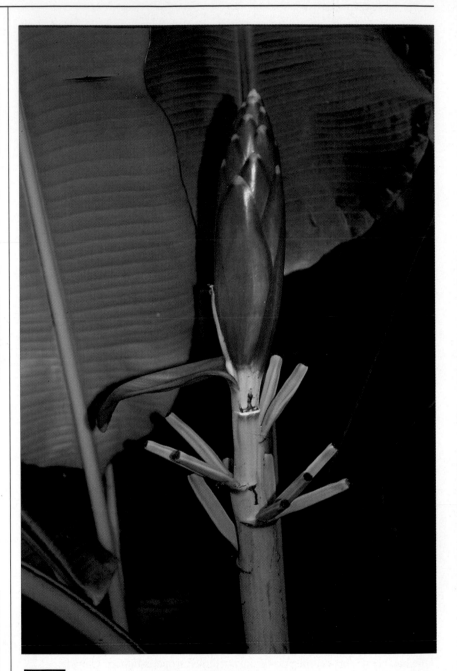

# THE SPECIES

## Quick View

### *Musa beccarii*

| | |
|---|---|
| **Type:** | S |
| **Height:** | 12 ft. (3.6 m) |
| **Form:** | M |
| **Zone:** | 8–10 |

**Remarks:**

Slender foliage.

Highly ornamental in flower.

Makes great cut flowers.

Excellent in containers and accent.

Seeded.

## FACTOID

Banana plants can grow as small as 2 ft. or soar to nearly 40 ft., depending on the species and cultivar.

This is a little known ornamental banana that is native to Borneo. The bracts are brilliant red with green tips. The small fruit is seeded and inedible. It is best suited to container growing in a protected site.

# THE SPECIES

## Quick View

*Musa mannii*
### Indian Dwarf Banana

| Type: | S |
|---|---|
| **Height:** | 2–4 ft. (.6–1.2 m) |
| **Form:** | M |
| **Zone:** | 8–10 |
| **Remarks:** | |
| Colorful in foliage and flower. | |
| Seeded species, fruit inedible. | |
| Dwarf size, excellent for containers. | |

## FACTOID

Bananas can grow as fast as 8 in. (20 cm) per day for a limited number of days.

This is a dwarf species from northeast India. The foliage is small for a banana, about 30 in. (75 cm) long by 8 in. (20 cm) wide. The inflorescence is an odd mix of crimson and purple-red. The pseudostem is deep brown to black. Very rarely grown, it has the potential for a colorful display in a container or protected spot. This species is rarely available but worth searching for. Great for small spaces, interiors, and warm gardens and as a conversation piece.

# THE SPECIES

## *Quick View*

*Musa ornata*
### 'Standard Lavender'
#### Ornamental Banana

| | |
|---|---|
| **Type:** | S |
| **Height:** | 5–12 ft. ( 1.6–3.6 m) |
| **Form:** | M |
| **Zone:** | 8–10 |
| **Remarks:** | |

Includes a number of varieties with colorful erect flowers and foliage.

Small seeded fruit are inedible.

Medium size in landscape or containers.

Large photo (1) shows a *Musa ornata* 'Standard Lavender' in bloom. The small photos inset from left to right are of (2) *Musa ornata* 'Costa Rican Stripe' and (3) *Musa ornata* 'Royal Burgundy.' Above photo shows ornamental fruit. Lower center photo (4) is of a *Musa ornata* 'Red Ruby' in bloom.

A highly ornamental small banana that is quite variable. *Musa ornata* 'Standard Lavender' is thought to be the original form from which the other colors have been selected. The inflorescence can be red-bronze, orange, lavender, pale pink, white, purple, or combinations of these colors. It is grown as a cut flower in Central and South America, but originates in Burma and Bangladesh. Small, ornamental fruits are also colorful and vary from green to red. Some named color forms are also shown. All may be grown as cut flowers. All bear fruits that are seeded and inedible. The short life cycle of 5–7 months usually results in flowers and fruit in one growing season.

# THE SPECIES

## Quick View

*Musa ornata*
### 'Leyte White'

🍌

### Ornamental Banana

🍌

| Type: | S |
|---|---|
| **Height:** | 5–10 ft. (1.6–3 m) |
| **Form:** | M |
| **Zone:** | 8–10 |

**Remarks:**

Fruit seeded and inedible

Medium size in landscape or containers.

Great in containers.

Similar to *Musa ornata* 'Standard Lavender' in appearance, but smaller and suckers well. Flower bracts make good cut flowers. Bracts are tight artichoke-like and tinged with magenta. The small, decorative, ivory bananas are inedible. May be named after Leyte Island in the Philippines. The plant will reach its upper limit of growth when planted in the ground in warm climates. Growth will be limited with planted in a container, given less light, or grown in cooler climate. A magnificent ornamental plant for small areas and containers.

# THE SPECIES

## *Quick View*

### *Musa ornata*
### 'Bronze'
### Ornamental Banana

| Type: | S |
|---|---|
| Height: | 5–10 ft. (1.6–3 m) |
| Form: | M |
| Zone: | 8–10 |

**Remarks:**

Typical size with bronze-orange bracts.

This form of the ornamental banana has bronze-orange bracts and bright yellow flowers. The foliage and stem have pink tones, which all match nicely.

In containers and in cooler climates, the height will only be around 5 ft. (1.6 m), but in the ground in a tropical climate it can get to an imposing 10 ft. (3 m).

Fruit seeded and inedible.

## *Quick View*

### *Musa ornata*
### 'Milky Way'
### Ornamental Banana

| Type: | S |
|---|---|
| Height: | 5–10 ft. (1.6–3 m) |
| Form: | M |
| Zone: | 8–10 |

**Remarks:**

Dark foliage with near-white bracts. Dramatic contrast.

Another form of ornamental banana with a dramatic contrast between the milky-white bracts against deep dark-green foliage.

Size and growth are similar to 'Bronze.'

Fruit seeded and inedible.

# THE SPECIES

## Quick View

*Musa ornata*
### 'Lavender Beauty'
**Ornamental Banana**

| | |
|---|---|
| **Type:** | S |
| **Height:** | 5–10 ft. (1.6–3 m) |
| **Form:** | M |
| **Zone:** | 8–10 |

**Remarks:**

Typical size.

Pink tones in stem. Pale pink-lavender bracts.

This form has paler foliage and stems with pink tones throughout.

Pale pink-lavender flowers followed by attractive, small dark-pink-to-crimson fruit.

Small seeded inedible fruit.

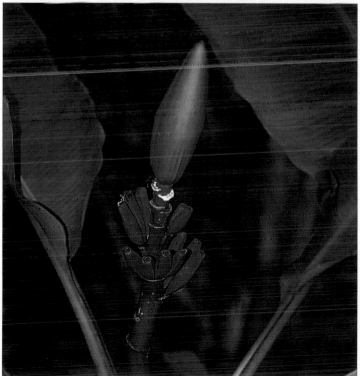

## Quick View

*Musa ornata*
### 'Royal Purple'
**Ornamental Banana**

| | |
|---|---|
| **Type:** | S |
| **Height:** | 5–10 ft. (1.6–3 m) |
| **Form:** | M |
| **Zone:** | 8–10 |

**Remarks:**

Typical size with richly colored bracts.

Landscape or containers.

The richly colored bracts have a definite blue-purple tinge. The plant has similar size and vigor of *Musa ornata* 'Bronze.'

Pale leaves and petioles show up well in the landscape or in containers.

Fruit seeded and inedible.

# THE SPECIES

## Quick View

### Musa textilis
### Abacá
### Manila Hemp
### Fiber Banana

| | |
|---|---|
| **Type:** | S |
| **Height:** | 25 ft. (7 m) |
| **Form:** | M |
| **Zone:** | 8–10 |

**Remarks:**

Fibers used in fabric and paper production.

Landscape accent.

Fruit is small with seeds and is inedible.

Pseudostem is slender and leaves are narrow and tapered.

### FACTOID

Dozens of tropical countries produce fabrics made from banana fibers.

This large species from the Philippines is still grown for fibers produced in the pseudostem and leaf petioles. The fibers are called Manila Hemp or Abacá and have many uses, such as cord used in fish nets, various fabrics, and papers. It now has a special use in hat making. Once widely grown, modern fabric and paper production have reduced its usage. The bracts are purple-red and produce inedible fruit. This is still a good landscape prospect in mild climates.

## THE SPECIES

### *Quick View*

*Musa uranoscopus*
*Syn. Musa coccinea*

**Red Flowering
Thai Banana**

**Thai Red Banana**

| | |
|---|---|
| Type: | S |
| **Height:** | 6–9 ft. (1.8 –2.7 m) |
| **Form:** | M |
| **Zone:** | 9–10 |
| **Remarks:** | |
| Best flowering. | |
| Containers and landscape. | |
| Seeded. | |

Photo by Maradee Cryer

Cut flowers of this species are appearing in flower markets all over the world.

A native to Thailand, Burma, Vietnam, and surrounding South-east Asia, the Thai Red Banana has the most beautiful inflo-rescence of any ornamental banana. The flower may be enjoyed for 5–6 months as it matures on the plant or as a cut flower lasting for several months. It is best grown in acid soils (pH 6.0 or less), and it tolerates some shade. The Latin name means "stargazer." Great in containers or massed in a tropical garden. Its small fruits are seeded and inedible.

# THE SPECIES

## Quick View

*Musa velutina*
### Hot Pink Banana

| | |
|---|---|
| **Type:** | S |
| **Height:** | 7 ft. (2.1 m) |
| **Form:** | M |
| **Zone:** | 7–10 |
| **Remarks:** | |

Best for containers.

Cold tolerant.

Reliable fruiting.

Patios, containers, and accent.

### FACTOID

The sap of most bananas causes dark stains on clothing. The sap of at least one species is used as an ink substitute.

One of the easiest and most available of ornamental bananas, it may prove hardy as far north as zone 6 with light protection. The red color in the pseudostems and petioles shows off the pink inflorescence. The small, velvety bright-pink fruit are produced in as few as 5–6 months. These inedible bananas split open when ripe to expose the many small, hard black seeds. These open fruits attract birds and small animals that eat them and spread the seed. A must for beginners and excellent in containers or in the ground.

# THE SPECIES

## Quick View

### *Musella lasiocarpa*

### Chinese Yellow Banana

| | |
|---|---|
| **Type:** | S |
| **Height:** | 6 ft. (1.8 m) or taller |
| **Form:** | E |
| **Zone:** | At least zone 7, but may prove hardier. |

**Remarks:**

Suckers readily, however suckers are tightly attached to "mother" pseudostem.

Large yellow, waxy bracts.

Excellent in landscapes and containers.

Recommended.

Seeded and inedible for humans; however all parts are used as pig food in China.

At one time this rare banana was thought to be extinct in the wild in its native Yunnan, China, home. Recently rediscovered and tissue cultured, plants are now widely available at low cost. Bright yellow, long-lasting, lotus-like flowers are the striking feature. Flowers may last up to 9 months on the plant. Because of its temperate origin, it may prove very hardy, but it remains to be widely tested. It produces small, fuzzy, rounded, nearly flat, seeded and inedible bananas. Highly recommended for unique flowers, foliage, and form. There may be another slightly different and as yet unnamed variety in cultivation.

# THE SPECIES

*Musella lasiocarpa* continued from previous page.

Planting of *Musella lasiocarpa* in China near Kumning in Yunnan Province (Used as food for pigs).

The common name of Yellow Lotus is obvious from this mass planting and especially in the closeup of the inflorescence. The small flowers and just-developing fruits can be seen in the unfolding bracts. The inflorescence can last for 6-9 months.

# THE CULTIVARS

Cultivars: The first name is our preferred cultivar name. Some popular banana varieties have been grown in many parts of the world and have been given a number of different names. Names that appear in single quotes are cultivars (see Glossary). Variety names can be quite confusing.

Type: There are three main types based on edibility and use. "D" stands for dessert bananas; these are the common sweet bananas and can be eaten raw. "P" is for plantain and other cooking bananas. These must be cooked usually while still green, before being eaten. "S" stands for species or seeded; these are generally inedible bananas used for ornamental or horticultural purposes.

Form: "E" refers to the *Ensete* form. These bananas have a short, thick trunk with a large upright- or outward-spreading crown of leaves. "M" refers to the typical *Musa* form. These have a taller trunk and horizontal or pendant foliage. Height may range from a few feet to large, tree-like heights.

Zone: This refers to USDA Hardiness Zones. See zone map on page 121. Minimum hardiness zone is given, however most will be hardy in warmer zones. Please refer to earlier comments on hardiness and expect flower and fruit production only in warmer parts of Zone 9 and warmer. In colder zones, these may be grown as ornamental and herbaceous perennials.

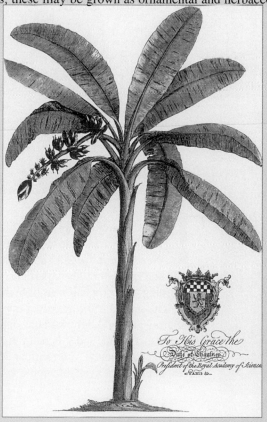

# THE CULTIVARS

## Quick View

### Musa
### 'Ae Ae'
### 'Koae'
### Hawaiian Varie-gated Banana

| | |
|---|---|
| **TYPE:** | D |
| **Height:** | 18 ft. (5.4 m) |
| **Form:** | M |
| **Zone:** | 9–10 |

**Remarks:**

Beautiful but demanding.

Prefers some shade, acid soil, and wind protection.

Variegated fruit of 'Ae Ae'.

This Hawaiian variety is the most colorful foliage banana available: a kaleidoscope of two-toned greens and whites. Needs some special care to show off to its best including an acid soil (pH 6.0 or less), partial shade to prevent drying, and sun burning, and protection from high winds; however worth the effort. The striped fruits are eaten raw or cooked like plantains. Once grown as food only for Hawaiian royalty. Tissue culture has not been successful, and it is naturally slow to propagate; therefore it is rare and expensive. The similar *Musa* 'Vittata' has narrower leaves, but it is not available commercially.

# THE CULTIVARS

## Quick View

*Musa*

### 'African Rhino Horn'
### 'Rhino Horn'

| | |
|---|---|
| **Type:** | D or P |
| **Height:** | 20 ft. (6 m) |
| **Form:** | M |
| **Zone:** | 9–10 |
| **Remarks:** | |
| Very large fruits. | |
| Attractive foliage. | |
| A conversation piece. | |

### FACTOID

Carmen Miranda, a Brazilian entertainer, is best known for her "banana extravaganza" in the movie *The Gang's All Here*.

This is a tall plantain with long, strongly curved fruits that give rise to its common name. This banana cultivar may have the longest fruits of any banana; up to 2 ft. (.7 m) in length, an individual fruit may weigh as much as 2 lbs. The colorful pseudostem and petioles make this an excellent landscaping plant, but too big for most containers. May be eaten ripe or cooked like other plantains.

# THE CULTIVARS

## Quick View

### Musa
### 'Bordelon'

| | |
|---|---|
| **Type:** | S |
| **Height:** | 9–14 ft. (2.8–4.3 m) |
| **Form:** | M |
| **Zone:** | 8–10 |
| **Remarks:** | |
| Rich color. | |
| Good hardiness. | |
| Great looks. | |

Inflorescence is neither erect nor pendant, but near horizonal.

First discovered in the Louisiana town of Bordelonville, this cultivar slightly resembles *Musa acuminata* ssp. zebrina, the Blood Banana. Large ornamental foliage has maroon splotches on the upper surface and even more maroon on the underside; this cultivar also grows taller so it has more impact. Readily produces flowers and makes seeded, inedible fruit, which are also ornamental. Makes an imposing colorful specimen, but has not yet been grown widely to test hardiness or suitability to other locations. A new cultivar to try widely. Now in tissue culture.

# THE CULTIVARS

*Quick View*

*Musa*
**'Brazilian'**
**'Brazilian Tall'**
**'Pome'**
**'Prata'**

| | |
|---|---|
| **Type:** | D |
| **Height:** | 20 ft. (6 m) |
| **Form:** | M |
| **Zone:** | 9–10 |
| **Remarks:** | |
| Extremely sweet fruit. | |
| Somewhat wind resistant. | |

O ne of the best landscaping cultivars for its tall size and wind resistance. Very popular also for its small bunches of extremely sweet, tasty fruit. It grows best in tropical climates in the ground where it can show off the green- and pink-tinted pseudostem and dark green foliage. Recommended.

# THE CULTIVARS

## Quick View

*Musa*

### 'Cardaba'
### 'Philippine Cardaba'

| | |
|---|---|
| **Type:** | P |
| **Height:** | 14 ft. (4.2 m) |
| **Form:** | M |
| **Zone:** | 8–10 |
| **Remarks:** | |

Good cooking plantain. See recipes.

Believed to be cultivar of 'Saba.'

One of best bananas for cooking. A beautiful plant with unusual bluish-green colored fruit. The bright white interior contrasts with the outer peel. A cultivar that is often recommended for making the Caribbean tostones (see "Recipes" in the last section of this book). Excellent cultivar.

# THE CULTIVARS

A super looking ornamental with huge dark green leaves, small ornamental bananas, and a very attractive globe-shaped male bud. Probably a hybrid of *Musa ornata*. Fruits are small, seeded and inedible.

Brun. Co. Master
Gardeners Assoc.
PO Box 109
Bolivia, NC 28422

Fruiting ornamental newly found and introduced from Costa Rica. May be a form of *Musa* 'Rose.' This banana is now being evaluated. Fruits are small, seeded and inedible.

# THE CULTIVARS

## Quick View

### Musa
### 'Double Banana'
### 'Mahoi'

| | |
|---|---|
| **Type:** | D |
| **Height:** | 7 ft. (2.1 m) |
| **Form:** | M |
| **Zone:** | 8–10 |
| **Remarks:** | |

Good for containers.

Excellent sweet fruit.

Conversation piece.

### FACTOID

An entire meal, from soup and salad through desserts and drinks, can be prepared from bananas and plantains!

Undoubtedly a sport or mutation of the common 'Dwarf Cavendish,' this cultivar routinely produces two large heads of fruit and can occasionally produce a third. The sweet fruit is highly rated, and it can be very productive. Rare and unusual. Grows like the *Musa acuminata* 'Dwarf Cavendish'.

# THE CULTIVARS

**Quick View**

*Musa*
**'Dwarf Brazilian'**

| | |
|---|---|
| **Type:** | D |
| **Height:** | 6–8 ft. ( 2–2.4 m) |
| **Form:** | M |
| **Zone:** | 8–10 |
| **Remarks:** | |
| Like 'Brazilian,' but much shorter. | |

V ery similar to the larger 'Brazilian,' but grows to only 1/3–1/2 the height. Its sweet bananas are also slightly smaller than the regular 'Brazilian.' It should be grown more widely, as it has good wind resistance and very tasty fruit. Its smaller stature makes it more suited to small gardens, greenhouses, and large containers.

# THE CULTIVARS

## Quick View

*Musa acuminata*
**'Dwarf
Cavendish'
'Canary Banana'
'Dwarf Chinese'
'Basrai'
'Petite Naine'
and others**

| | |
|---|---|
| **Type:** | D |
| **Height:** | 6–7 ft. (1.8–2 m) |
| **Form:** | M |
| **Zone:** | 8–10 |
| **Remarks:** | |
| Overall excellent. | |
| Containers, greenhouse. | |
| Recommended. | |

The term "dwarf banana" does not refer to any specific cultivar although the 'Dwarf Cavendish' is the most common cultivar. Commercial bananas in the "dwarf" size range (from 6 to 10 ft. or less) are ideal for ease of cultivation and harvest. Traditional older cultivars of commercial bananas grew to over 10 ft. and made harvesting difficult. Tall banana plants also tend to become top heavy when full of fruit, and entire bunches could be lost in high winds or storms. Most commercial cultivars are now "dwarf bananas."

This is one of the best bananas for many locations. It was once a very popular commercial variety and is still widely grown. The plant is dwarf-sized, but it produces large bunches of medium-sized sweet fruit. Does well in greenhouses, containers, and winters well indoors in northern climates. This cultivar had numerous origins since it is a naturally occuring dwarf mutant of taller members of the 'Cavendish' family. It is widely available, low priced and recommended.

# THE CULTIVARS

## Quick View

### Musa
### 'Dwarf Kalapua'

| | |
|---|---|
| **Type:** | P |
| **Height:** | less than 12 ft. (3.6 m) |
| **Form:** | M |
| **Zone:** | 9–10 |
| **Remarks:** | |

Colorful bracts and small size offer potential for smaller gardens.

Very attractive inflorescence.

This is a new cultivar in the United States. Originally from Papua, New Guinea, it was recently introduced by the University of Florida in Homestead. It is not yet widely grown in cultivation. The fruits may become sweet enough when ripe to be eaten raw as a dessert banana. Colorful flowers, small size, and possible dual-fruit usage suggest it may have value in the home garden where space is limited. Deserves to be more widely grown and tested for taste and hardiness. It is believed to be vigorous and drought tolerant, but needs more testing.

# THE CULTIVARS

## Quick View

*Musa*
**'Dwarf Orinoco'**
**'Dwarf Bluggoe'**
**'Chamaluco Enano'**

| | |
|---|---|
| **Type:** | D and P |
| **Height:** | 6–7 ft. (1.8–2 m) |
| **Form:** | M |
| **Zone:** | 8–10 |

**Remarks:**

Deserves to be grown more widely. Overall excellent.

Fruits are very angular.

Another dwarf cultivar of a popular banana. Like 'Orinoco,' it is both wind and cold resistant. It tolerates a wide range of conditions and is suited to smaller gardens, containers, and greenhouses. It is a heavy bearer of thick-skinned fruit that can be eaten fresh when ripe or cooked when green. This cultivar has just become available in commerce, and it should be tested in more places.

# THE CULTIVARS

### Quick View

*Musa*
## 'Dwarf Puerto Rican'

| | |
|---|---|
| **Type:** | P |
| **Height:** | 6–8 ft. (1.8–2.4 m) |
| **Form:** | M |
| **Zone:** | 8-10 |
| **Remarks:** | |

Smaller plantain with preferred taste and quality.

This smaller cultivar is considered by many to be among the best of all plantain types. It is widely grown in Puerto Rico for its preferred taste and cooking qualities. Most plantain types are tall growing, so this is an exception. Its small size also makes it worth trying.

### FACTOID

Bananas were brought to the Middle East and Africa in the second century by Arab traders.

# THE CULTIVARS

## Quick View
QV

*Musa*
**'Dwarf Red'**
**'Dwarf Cuban'**
**'Dwarf Jamaican'**

| | |
|---|---|
| **Type:** | D |
| **Height:** | 6–8 ft. (1.8–2.4 m) |
| **Form:** | M |
| **Zone:** | 8–10 |

**Remarks:**

Plant and fruits show beautiful red/yellow colors.

A great looking plant easily recognizable from a distance.

O ne of many red-skinned banana cultivars, this one stays short and takes up little space. Most red bananas are much esteemed for good tasting fruit, and this one is no exception. This cultivar also has red pseudostems. A favorite small banana, the red bananas take longer to ripen than most. The skin should be almost black before it is ripe enough to eat.

## FACTOID

Technically the banana fruit is a berry with a pericarp.

# THE CULTIVARS

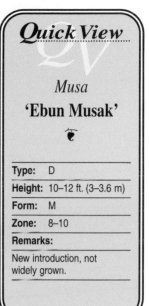

**Quick View**

*Musa*
**'Ebun Musak'**

| | |
|---|---|
| **Type:** | D |
| **Height:** | 10–12 ft. (3–3.6 m) |
| **Form:** | M |
| **Zone:** | 8–10 |
| **Remarks:** | |

New introduction, not widely grown.

One of the few banana cultivars introduced from Borneo. Oddly, the fruit is still green when ripe; its flavor is very nice with a slightly sharp taste. The plant produces very colorful pseudostems and petioles. It's not very widely grown, so some features are not fully appreciated. One to try in new locations.

# THE CULTIVARS

## Quick View
### QV

*Musa*
**'Ele Ele'**
**'Black Hawaiian'**

| | |
|---|---|
| **Type:** | P |
| **Height:** | 20–25 ft. (6–7.5 m) |
| **Form:** | M |
| **Zone:** | 8–10 |

**Remarks:**

Blackish pseudostem, petioles, midribs; leaves green.

Good grower.

An all-around excellent choice for tropical climates because of the dramatic near-black blotches of pseudostem and petioles. A tall cultivar suited to making its mark in the tropical landscape. Large bunches of fruit are produced. The fruits are not black, but green at first and then yellow like most cultivars; the flesh is tinted orange. This vigorous plant is a recommended collector's cultivar that was once restricted to use by Hawaiian royalty.

# THE CULTIVARS

## *Quick View*

*Musa*
**'FHIA-01'**
**'Goldfinger'**

| | |
|---|---|
| **Type:** | D |
| **Height:** | 14 ft. (4.3 m) |
| **Form:** | M |
| **Zone:** | 8–10 |

**Remarks:**

New hybrid commercial variety.

High wind and disease resistant

Great tasting fruit.

---

**FACTOID**
·····················

Until the 19th century, Hawaiian women were forbidden to eat bananas.

---

A recent product of the banana breeding program in Honduras, this cultivar has commercial potential. It is just recently available for home gardening. It has high wind resistance, some cold tolerance, and excellent disease resistance with a strong pseudostem and base. It is an outstanding producer of delicious tasting bananas that are reminiscent of one of its parents, *Musa* 'Dwarf Prata'. This new cultivar should be tried in all conditions.

# THE CULTIVARS

**Quick View**
*QV*

*Musa*
**'FHIA-03'**
**'Sweetheart'**

| | |
|---|---|
| **Type:** | D & P |
| **Height:** | 10–12 ft. (3–3.6 m) |
| **Form:** | M |
| **Zone:** | 9–10 |
| **Remarks:** | |

New potential commercial cultivar with increased disease resistance.

**FACTOID**

The Annual Banana Festival (part of the "Weekend at Pontotoc") held in September in Fulton, Kentucky, attracts thousands of visitors and more than 10,000 tons of fruit are consumed. For information, look up www.wkynet.com/FultonNet/pontotoc.html

The FHIA is a federal organization that is owned by the Honduran government. It has been breeding bananas for forty years. Their first widely available cultivar, *Musa* hybrid 'FHIA-01' ('Goldfinger'), is already having some impact and this new hybrid is sure to follow. *Musa* hybrid 'FHIA-03' ('Sweetheart') was bred and selected for increased disease resistance and yield. Excellent flavor and good size make it attractive to the home gardener. It is only recently available.

# THE CULTIVARS

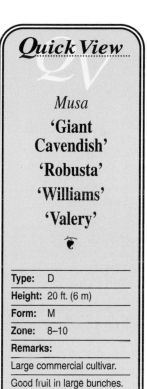

*Quick View*

*Musa*
**'Giant Cavendish'**
**'Robusta'**
**'Williams'**
**'Valery'**

| | |
|---|---|
| **Type:** | D |
| **Height:** | 20 ft. (6 m) |
| **Form:** | M |
| **Zone:** | 8–10 |
| **Remarks:** | |

Large commercial cultivar.
Good fruit in large bunches.

Like other 'Cavendish' types, this is a commercial cultivar that produces large bunches of high-quality fruit. It is a tall grower, but its lack of wind resistance has caused it to be replaced by newer shorter types. Grow in a protected site. This cultivar is great in the landscape.

# THE CULTIVARS

## Quick View
*QV*

*Musa*
**'Grand Nain'**
**'Grande Naine'**
**'Umalog'**

🍌

| | |
|---|---|
| **Type:** | D |
| **Height:** | 8 ft. (2.4 m) |
| **Form:** | M |
| **Zone:** | 8–10 |
| **Remarks:** | |
| Common commercial variety in Central America. | |
| Good for landscape. | |
| Wind resistant. | |

Still the mostly widely grown commercial banana in the world today. If it is a "Chiquita," it is probably this cultivar. Bunches may weigh up to 150 lbs. (60 kg). It is also a nice landscape plant and has good wind resistance. The medium-height plant is suited to landscape and containers; however, it is not as cold tolerant as some other cultivars.

## THE CULTIVARS

**Quick View**

*Musa*
'Gros Michel'
'Pisang Embun'
'Bluefields'

| | |
|---|---|
| **Type:** | D |
| **Height:** | 12 ft. (3.6 m) |
| **Form:** | M |
| **Zone:** | 8–10 |
| **Remarks:** | |

Once the commercial cultivar of dessert bananas.

This used to be the primary cultivar in world of banana commerce. It has been replaced by 'Grand Nain,' 'Giant Cavendish,' and other cultivars with better disease, wind and cold resistance. It is now seldom grown except in northeast Ecuador. It is still an acceptable home-garden cultivar with good flavor.

**FACTOID**

The little girl said, "I know how to spell 'banana,' but I don't know when to stop."

# THE CULTIVARS

## Quick View

*Musa*
**'Huamoa'**

| | |
|---|---|
| **Type:** | P |
| **Height:** | 10–12 ft. (3–3.6 m) |
| **Form:** | M |
| **Zone:** | 8–10 |

**Remarks:**

One of the best bananas for cooking.

Oddly shaped short and thick fruits.

This is another exceptional Hawaiian cultivar recommended for beginners. It is an excellent cooking banana adaptable to many cooking styles. The bunches are smaller than most varieties, but the odd individual fruits are up to 4 in. (10 cm) in diameter; some fruits are equally short, hardly looking like bananas at all. They often grow up to 10 in. long. A related Hawaiian cultivar, *Musa* hybrid 'Moa,' has more, but smaller fruits. It is also related to the cultivar *Musa* 'Popoulu.' Recommended.

# THE CULTIVARS

## *Quick View*

*Musa*
### 'Ice Cream'
### 'Blue Java'
### 'Ney Mannan'

| | |
|---|---|
| **Type:** | D and P |
| **Height:** | 15 ft. (4.5 m) |
| **Form:** | M |
| **Zone:** | 8–10 |

**Remarks:**

Beautiful fruit, rated best tasting by many.

Good cooking banana.

A great banana for many reasons. Many consider this the best tasting of all bananas and compare its flavor to that of vanilla custard or ice cream. Highly regarded. The skins have an odd, silvery-blue sheen and then ripen to a pale canary-yellow color. A bit tall, but otherwise well suited to the home garden and the greenhouse. May be a bit large for containers.

# THE CULTIVARS

*Musa*
**'Kru'**

| | |
|---|---|
| **Type:** | D |
| **Height:** | 10–12 ft. (3–3.6 m) |
| **Form:** | M |
| **Zone:** | 8–10 |
| **Remarks:** | |

Sturdy plant highly rated for good taste. Very attractive.

Another highly rated banana for excellent taste. This import from New Guinea deserves to be more widely grown by the home gardener. This is also a very colorful banana fruit with deep shades of red on the pseudostem; the bananas are a mix of red and green shades. This is a very distinctive banana cultivar and can easily be recognized from a distance. A sturdy plant suited to home gardens and the greenhouse and well suited to containers.

## THE CULTIVARS

*Quick View*

*Musa*
**'Monkey Fingers'**
**'Pisang jari buaya'**

| | |
|---|---|
| **Type:** | D |
| **Height:** | 20 ft. (6 m) |
| **Form:** | M |
| **Zone:** | 8–10 |
| **Remarks:** | |
| Long bunch of fruit with small skinny fruits. Unique. | |
| A conversation piece. | |

The "finger bananas" are those with small, narrow finger-shaped fruits. This tall cultivar is known for the long bunch of bananas that it produces. These bunches can be six feet long and weigh 75 to 80 lbs. The hands of bananas are widely separated. The flavor is tart and not especially tasty. It is mostly grown because of its' disease resistance and it has been used in the FHIA breeding program. It is a real conversation piece in the garden or greenhouse, and its large size makes it valuable for land-scaping.

# THE CULTIVARS

**Quick View**

*Musa*

'Mysore'
'Poovan'
'Embul'
"Pisang Keling'
'Pisang Ceylon'

| Type: | D |
|---|---|
| **Height:** | 16 ft. (4.8 m) |
| **Form:** | M |
| **Zone:** | 8–10 |
| **Remarks:** | |

Indian cultivar with many small, very tasty fruit.

Wind and disease resistant.

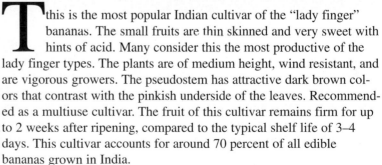

Characteristic pinkish undersides of leaves in young plants.

This is the most popular Indian cultivar of the "lady finger" bananas. The small fruits are thin skinned and very sweet with hints of acid. Many consider this the most productive of the lady finger types. The plants are of medium height, wind resistant, and are vigorous growers. The pseudostem has attractive dark brown colors that contrast with the pinkish underside of the leaves. Recommended as a multiuse cultivar. The fruit of this cultivar remains firm for up to 2 weeks after ripening, compared to the typical shelf life of 3–4 days. This cultivar accounts for around 70 percent of all edible bananas grown in India.

# THE CULTIVARS

*Quick View*

*Musa*
**'Namwah'**
**'Kluai Namwa'**
**'Pisang Awak'**

| | |
|---|---|
| **Type:** | D & P |
| **Height:** | 10–14 ft. (3–4 m) |
| **Form:** | M |
| **Zone:** | 9–10 |
| **Remarks:** | |

Fruit has excellent flavor with yellow pulp.

This banana from Thailand is the most commonly grown cultivar in that country. It is highly regarded for its flavor, but it is widespread in cultivation due to its drought resistance and vigor. In a country such as Thailand, that is subject to monsoon rains and a long dry season, these are important characteristics. The colorful bracts are an ornamental plus.

# THE CULTIVARS

## Quick View

*Musa*
**'Orinoco'**
**'Bluggoe'**
**'Burro'**
**'Largo'**

| | |
|---|---|
| **Type:** | D and P |
| **Height:** | 17–21 ft. (5.8–6.3 m) |
| **Form:** | M |
| **Zone:** | 7–10 |
| **Remarks:** | |
| Relatively cold hardy. | |
| Common on the U.S. Gulf Coast. | |
| Excellent reliable fruit. | |

A nearly ideal banana for many locations. The plant is vigorous and produces large clumps of wind-resistant foliage and a very tropical landscape effect. The fruit is multiuse and may be eaten ripe or cooked while green. Its distinct, angular fruits are produced regularly in zone 9 and may prove even hardier. This is the common street and garden banana in New Orleans and is widely grown along the Gulf Coast, south Florida, and Cuba.

## THE CULTIVARS

### *Quick View*

*Musa*
**'Pisang Raja'**
**'Grindy'**

| | |
|---|---|
| **Type:** | D & P |
| **Height:** | 16 ft. (5 m) |
| **Form:** | M |
| **Zone:** | 8–10 |
| **Remarks:** | |
| Large fruits. | |
| Relatively cold and wind resistant. | |

The name 'Pisang' simply means "banana" in Indonesia and Malaysia where this cultivar is very common and believed to have originated. This is a large landscape cultivar with good cold and wind tolerance. The fruit has a slightly fuzzy feel and the taste is said to be "divine." Not as widely grown and tested in home gardens as it should be, it is worth trying further north.

# THE CULTIVARS

## Quick View
### QV

*Musa*
### 'Pitogo'

| | |
|---|---|
| **Type:** | D |
| **Height:** | 12 ft. (3.6 m) |
| **Form:** | M |
| **Zone:** | 8–10 |
| **Remarks:** | |
| Unusual, nearly round fruit. | |
| Excellent flavor. | |
| Philippine cultivar. | |

One of the more unusual bananas with small nearly-round fruit ranging in size and shape from golf balls to tennis balls. The fruit is very tasty and each make up a couple of small bites. Dark green throughout, this banana plant is of medium size and is otherwise undistinguished. Often listed as a collector's plant.

# THE CULTIVARS

*Quick View*

*Musa*
**'Popoulu'**

| Type: | D and P |
|---|---|
| **Height:** | 14 ft. (4.2 m) |
| **Form:** | M |
| **Zone:** | 8–10 |
| **Remarks:** | |

Pink-fleshed fruit with dual usage.

Hawaiian origin.

his Hawaiian cultivar can be eaten or cooked green. The fruits are stocky and have an unusual flesh with a mild taste reminiscent of apples. The Hawaiian name means "ball-shaped like breadfruit." This cultivar is related to *Musa* 'Huamoa', which has the roundest fruits in this group. See also *Musa* 'Pitogo', a round Phillipine cultivar.

# THE CULTIVARS

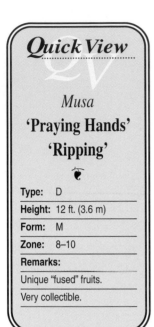

## Quick View

### Musa
### 'Praying Hands'
### 'Ripping'

| | |
|---|---|
| **Type:** | D |
| **Height:** | 12 ft. (3.6 m) |
| **Form:** | M |
| **Zone:** | 8–10 |
| **Remarks:** | |
| Unique "fused" fruits. | |
| Very collectible. | |

This produces perhaps the most unusual and distinctive of all banana fruits. Two adjacent hands of bananas are fused, giving the appearance of praying hands. Not just a collector's item, the fruits are delicious ripe, containing a hint of vanilla flavor. When totally ripe, individual bananas can be carefully separated from each other. An excellent all-around plant with some wind resistance; it is very collectible.

# THE CULTIVARS

## *Quick View*

### *Musa* 'Rajapuri'

| | |
|---|---|
| **Type:** | D |
| **Height:** | 8–10 ft. (2.4–3 m) |
| **Form:** | M |
| **Zone:** | 8–10 |
| **Remarks:** | |
| Top choice for home land-scape. | |
| Wind and cold resistant. | |

Often recommended for beginners, this banana has it all. It is very resistant to wind, cold and some diseases; however it is extremely susceptible to Black Sigatoka and is no longer recommended in South Florida due to this problem. Because it fruits readily in many climates and has very good-flavored medium-sized fruits, it is still a good choice in other parts of the U.S. It can flower in as little as nine months. It is a popular banana in India and for first time growers. Recommended and nearly fool proof !

# THE CULTIVARS

## Quick View

*Musa*
**'Red'**

| | |
|---|---|
| **Type:** | D |
| **Height:** | 16–18 ft. (5–5.4 m) |
| **Form:** | M |
| **Zone:** | 8–10 |
| **Remarks:** | |
| A tall red-fruited banana. | |
| Beautiful in fruit. | |

S imilar to *Musa* 'Green Red', but with the red color found in the flowers and fruit and, to a lesser degree, on the petioles and pseudostems. The fruits are also similar: green and gold when ripe, pulp is aromatic and creamy orange in color. This red color selection will occasionally revert to all green and is known then a *Musa* 'Green Red'. Takes twenty to thirty months to produce its first fruit, but produces annually thereafter.

# THE CULTIVARS

## Quick View

*Musa*
**'Red Iholene'**
**'Hawaiian Red'**

| | |
|---|---|
| **Type:** | D and P |
| **Height:** | 12 ft. (3.6 m) |
| **Form:** | M |
| **Zone:** | 8–10 |

**Remarks:** One of the most beautiful of all bananas. Distinctive!

Most commonly used for cooking.

One of the most ornamental of all banana plants, and this one bears fine-tasting fruit, too. This Hawaiian cultivar has leaves that are burgundy colored on their lower surface to match the red-pink pseudostem. Being of a modest height, it is suited to both the landscape and greenhouse where it makes a beautiful specimen. The unripe fruit skin starts out pale yellow and should not be picked until it is totally and really ripe. This is a close relative of *Musa* 'White Iholene' and *Musa* 'Ha'a,' which is the dwarf form of the 'Iholene' group.

# THE CULTIVARS

## Quick View

### Musa
### 'Rose'

| | |
|---|---|
| **Type:** | D |
| **Height:** | 12–14 ft. *(3.6-4.2 m)* |
| **Form:** | M |
| **Zone:** | 9–11 |

**Remarks:**

Very distinctive pseudostems, small ornamental fruit, and nice looking inflorescense that grows somewhat horizonally.

The cultivar *Musa* 'Rose' originated in Indonesia. Although the pseudostem color and ornamental foliage can be appreciated, this is an edible banana. It has been used by French hybridizers in their banana breeding programs. This cultivar is widely grown in tropical and subtropical areas of the world, but not widely grown in gardens.

# THE CULTIVARS

## Quick View

### Musa
### 'Saba'
### 'Pisang Kepok'
### 'Pisang Abu Nipak'

| Type: | D and P. |
|---|---|
| Height: | 17–21 ft. (5.2–6.4 m) |
| Form: | M |
| Zone: | 8–10 |

**Remarks:**

Large plant with good cold and wind tolerance.

Mainly used for cooking

Good shade provider.

This large plant is often grown just for shade in its native Philippines. It is widely grown in Indonesia and Malaysia. The overall green color suggests a sturdy quality that agrees with its cold tolerance and wind resistance. Its dual-use fruit can be eaten cooked or ripe. It does best in the landscape or in a large greenhouse. At maturity, this cultivar can form a huge base up to 24 in. in diameter.

# THE CULTIVARS

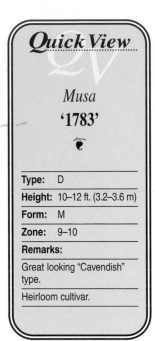

### Quick View

*Musa*
**'1783'**

| Type: | D |
|---|---|
| **Height:** | 10–12 ft. (3.2–3.6 m) |
| **Form:** | M |
| **Zone:** | 9–10 |
| **Remarks:** | |
| Great looking "Cavendish" type. | |
| Heirloom cultivar. | |

The '1783' has a very tasty edible fruit. The significance of this plant is that its origin can be traced back to Haiti on the island of Hispaniola. In 1783 Mr. Claude Tremé brought the banana to his large plantation along the Mississippi River just below the present French Quarter in New Orleans. In 1993 banana plants from this original location in Louisiana were transplanted to Laura Plantation in St. James Parish (40 miles up the Mississippi River above New Orleans, Louisiana) where it has florished since. So this is a banana planting in which we know the provenance going back to 1783.

# THE CULTIVARS

## Quick View

*Musa*
'Super Dwarf Cavendish'
'Dwarf Parfitt'
'Dwarf Nathan'

| | |
|---|---|
| **Type:** | D |
| **Height:** | 4 ft. (1.2 m) |
| **Form:** | M |
| **Zone:** | 8–10 |

**Remarks:**

Smallest banana; has tiny edible fruit.

Great in containers or even as a ground cover.

This *Musa* 'Super Dwarf Cavendish' with variegated foliage was found as a tissue culture sport. It is not yet available commercially.

One of the "hottest" new bananas around, it is small enough to grow in a gallon pot or as a ground cover, in a patio container, or the smallest greenhouse. It may produce tasty mini-bananas. Its *Musa* 'Cavendish' parentage ensures disease, wind, and cold resistance in the landscape or as a houseplant. This is the one that will amaze your friends. It has to be tried to be believed.

# THE CULTIVARS

## Quick View

*Musa*

**'Thousand Fingers'**
**'Pisang Seribu'**
**'Kluai Roi Wi'**

| | |
|---|---|
| **Type:** | D |
| **Height:** | 10–12 ft. (3.2–3.6 m) |
| **Form:** | M |
| **Zone:** | 8–10 |
| **Remarks:** | |
| Can produce hundreds of small, sweet fruit. | |

Another finger banana, this is a sturdy plant that produces a large number of tiny 1-1/2 in. (3.5 cm) long sweet fruits. The banana bunch can be up to 10 ft. long and consist of hundreds of fruits. This is not just a specimen for collectors, but a good producer of fruit as well. It is a great conversation piece when in fruit.

# THE CULTIVARS

## *Quick View*
QV

*Musa*
**'Veinte Cohol'**

| Type: | D |
|---|---|
| **Height:** | 10–12 ft. (3.2–3.6 m) |
| **Form:** | M |
| **Zone:** | 8–10 |
| **Remarks:** | |

Produces small, sweet high-qualtiy fruit.

Vigorous growth.

This is a Phillipine cultivar of dessert banana. The name translates roughly as "Twenty Shoots" suggesting vigorous suckering. This variety has thin-skinned fruits that are golden-yellow when ripe. They are esteemed for their sweet flavor. It has relatively small bunches and thus smaller yield than some cultivars. It should be grown more for home use.

# THE CULTIVARS

## *Quick View*
QV

*Musa*
**'White Iholene'**
**'Hawaiian White'**

| | |
|---|---|
| **Type:** | D and P |
| **Height:** | 14–16 ft. (4.4–4.8 m) |
| **Form:** | M |
| **Zone:** | 8–10 |
| **Remarks:** | |

Pale plant with fruits that are orange when ripe.

Cold sensitive.

This relative of *Musa* 'Red Iholene' is also from Hawaii. The waxy coating gives a white appearance to the pseudostem. The fruit matures very rapidly—as quick as 7–8 weeks from flowering. The pulp of the fruit ripens to an orange color. The fruit can be cooked when green or eaten ripe. Somewhat cold sensitive, it is well suited to tropical climates. *Musa* 'Ha'a' is a dwarf form of this cultivar.

# THE CULTIVARS

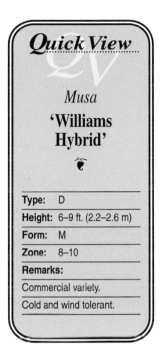

*Quick View*

*Musa*

**'Williams Hybrid'**

| | |
|---|---|
| **Type:** | D |
| **Height:** | 6–9 ft. (2.2–2.6 m) |
| **Form:** | M |
| **Zone:** | 8–10 |
| **Remarks:** | |
| Commercial variety. | |
| Cold and wind tolerant. | |

This banana, *Musa* hybrid 'Williams Hybrid', is obviously a different much-shorter form of 'Williams' or 'Giant Cavendish'. It bears large bunches of good-tasting fruit. It is similar to other members of the *Musa* hybrid 'Cavendish' group of closely related cultivars. Like most of them, it has cold and wind resistance. It is also grown commercially, but in the home garden, it is a good source of excellent sweet dessert bananas.

# THE CULTIVARS

## Quick View

*Musa*
**Zan Moreno**

| | |
|---|---|
| **Type:** | D |
| **Height:** | 6–8 ft. (2.2–2.5 m) |
| **Form:** | M |
| **Zone:** | 8–10 |
| **Remarks:** | |
| New cultivar. | |

This is another of the *Musa* 'Dwarf Cavendish' group of cultivars. It shares many basic characteristics: small size, high-quality fruit, some disease and cold resistance. This cultivar has not been widely grown in the U.S. and should do as well as others in this group. Colorful bracts and maroon stains on short broad foliage. One to be tried for better understanding of its use in home gardens.

*Part IV*

# ESSENTIAL INFORMATION

Antique print of *Musa coccinea* (now correctly known as *Musa uranoscopus*) by P.J. Redouté, French, 1759-1840.

Recipes

Hardiness Zone Map

Best Lists

# GLOSSARY

CULTIVAR—Simply a "cultivated variety"; that is, any plant selected for some special characteristic and brought into cultivation. According to the rules of naming cultivars, the plant should have a name with a capital first letter and be in single quotes, such as 'Cavendish.'

DIPLOID—Plant or a cell having two sets of chromosomes. All banana species have two sets of chromosomes. This is written as "2n." There are also banana hybrids with three or four sets of chromosomes; see triploid and tetraploid.

GENUS/GENERA—Plants are given scientific names. The scientific name consists of two parts: the genus (or general) name and the species (or specific) name, such as *Musa acuminata* or *Musa velutina*. The genus is composed of related species, such as the two *Musa* species named above. All species in the genus *Musa* are more closely related to each other than any plants in another genus, such as *Ensete* or *Musella*.

The word "genera" is simply the plural form of the word "genus." All scientific names are in Latin and, according to the rules of English grammar, should be printed in italics or underlined, with the first letter of the genus capitalized.

HARDINESS ZONE—The United States Department of Agriculture (USDA) has researched weather information for all of the continental United States. These data have been expressed as zones of plant hardiness based on average winter low temperatures with each zone expressed as 10°F (4-1/2°C) of temperature. See map in the Appendix on page 121.

HARDY—The quality of enduring and surviving low temperatures and other climatic extremes. Usually this refers to surviving extreme temperatures below freezing, but can be a relative term to describe certain plants that are more hardy than others. There are many factors that combine to make one plant hardier than another. These include resistance to wind, cold, drying, and the plant's own genetic and physical characteristics. It should be pointed out that all bananas are tropical and/or subtropical plants so hardiness is relative. Some bananas and cultivars are more cold tolerant, or hardier, than others.

Bananas can not flower or fruit if they are exposed to below freezing temperatures as this will kill the developing flower. Even a short period of below freezing temperatures during a crucial stage of development will kill the emerging flowers or fruit. Fruiting is only insured if plants are kept from freezing at all stages in this cycle of development.

Many banana species and cultivars will still survive above ground after freezing, even if there is leaf damage. The greater the damage to the leaves, petioles, or pseudostem, the greater the chance that plant will not survive above ground. Some bananas will survive as underground rhizomes even when the plant is frozen to the ground. Generally these species will not fruit unless they have a very short growth, flower, and fruit cycle such as *Musa velutina* and others. These can be enjoyed as ornamental herbaceous perennials.

MAT—After a banana plant has produced fruit and multiplied with a number of suckers, the collective planting of mature and immature plants is called a mat. All plants in the mat come from a single original plant. This term refers to the whole plant group or clump.

MERISTEM—The growing point of a plant that is comprised of a small number of actively dividing undifferentiated cells. The meristem is a specialized tissue that develops all of a plant's new growth. In plants such as bananas where there is a single meristem, that structure is found buried deep within the plant until fruiting occurs. In woody trees, there can be many meristems.

MICROPROPAGATION—Any of many related technical practices to propagate a plant using very small portions of the "mother plant." Tissue culture is one form of micropropagation as is bulb scaling (using a small portion of a bulb to produce dozens of new bulbs from one "mother bulb").

MIDRIB—The central raised portion in the middle of most leaves. Each leaf has three main parts: the petiole, the blade or leaf surface, and the midrib. The midrib gives support and structure to the blade and houses the transport system for movement of water and nutrients to and from the leaf blade.

PARTHENOCARPY—The development of a ripe fruit without fertilization of the ovules; no seeds are produced. Triploidy in bananas also results in parthenocarpic fruit production: seedless bananas.

PETIOLE—The individual leaf stalk. Usually a petiole is attached to a stem, but in the banana plant the petioles are tightly inter-wrapped to form the pseudostem and instead attach directly to the large underground rhizome.

pH—An independent measure of acidity based on the number and quality of hydrogen ions in a sample. The neutral situation is based on a pH of 7.0. A pH below this number is considered acid, such as pH 6, pH 5, etc., while a pH above 7.0 is alkaline with alkalinity increasing as the pH rises. Bananas grow best in slightly acid soils with a pH around 6.5, but some prefer a lower pH (6.0 or less) and a few can tolerate higher alkalinity of 8 and more, but these levels of alkalinity are to be avoided for best growth.

PLANTAIN—Common name for any banana that is best eaten after cooking. Some cultivars will ripen sufficiently to be sweet and edible raw, but others can cause stomach upset and distress if eaten raw. True plantains are a specific subgroup of bananas that are utilized primarily as a cooked food such as *Musa* 'African Rhino Horn'. Cooking bananas are all other types that are usually cooked before eating such as *Musa* 'Cardaba'.

Plantains are an important starch in the diets of millions of people in tropical countries around the world. Generally plantains have more fibrous fruits with starches not fully converted to sugars.

POLYPLOID—Just as a diploid plant has two sets of chromosomes, a polyploid has multiple sets. Natural or man-made hybrids may have three (triploid) or four (tetraploid) sets of chromosomes, but plants with higher chromosome numbers may show aberrations in morphology and weak constitutions.

PSEUDOSTEM—This term essentially means "false stem" as the psedu-ostem of the banana is composed of the tightly inter-wrapped petioles from the leaves of the banana. The pseudostem is often, but incorrectly, called the trunk or stem. In bananas, the true stem develops only as the plant flowers.

RHIZOME—The specialized underground part of a plant modified for food storage. The rhizome is generally a horizontal, branched, underground stem such as that found in gingers, heliconias, cannas, and other related families. In the banana plant the rhizome is highly modified, and there is some techni-cal dispute over whether this is a true rhizome or not. Some authors will refer to the banana rhizome as a "corm." Roots grow out from rhizomes.

TISSUE CULTURE—This is a specialized technique of micropropagation that is widely used in many plants, and is also very useful in bananas. The general technique involves growing a few cells isolated from a plant's meris-tem. This small piece of plant material is cleaned under sterile conditions. Then it is placed on a sterile nutrient medium and allowed to grow. The chemical makeup of this medium consists of vitamins, fertilizers, hormones, and other plant stimulants. By varying the balance of these ingredients, the meristem can be made to produce more meristems, roots, and/or other struc-tures. Using this scientific procedure, it is possible to grow hundreds of new plants from one single "mother plant" in the course of a few months' time. Commercial banana growers can purchase hundreds or thousands of geneti-cally identical, superior tissue-cultured and disease-free plants all growing at the same stage of development. The grower can plant new plantations of essentially identical plants. This makes care and watering much easier, and the bananas will tend to be more synchronous in producing flowers and fruits for ease of harvesting. Tissue-cultured plants have greatly reduced the cost of propagation and made even rare varieties readily available at lower prices to the gardener.

TETRAPLOID—In the course of genetic variation, the normal diploid set of chromosomes may double. This double condition is called a tetraploid. Tetraploid plants may exhibit a number of special features. In bananas, tetraploidy has produced hybrids with superior fruits. *Musa* hybrids 'FHIA-01' and FHIA-03' are tetraploid hybrids. This is written as 4n.

TRIPLOID—This is a similar situation to the tetraploid condition defined above except triploid plants will have only three sets of chromosomes. Triploid bananas may combine more superior genetic features, but also have a greater chance of sterility. It is likely that the earliest edible bananas were natural sterile hybrids between two diploid species that produced a sterile triploid with edible fruit and no seeds. Most of the naturally occurring banana cultivars are triploids. Since triploids often have superior plant archi-tecture, fruit quality and yield, it is thought that ancient man selected these clones over the new less prevalent diploid and tetraploid cultivars. This is written as 3n.

# Best Bananas

## THE BASIC BANANA COLLECTION

The following list of bananas forms a basic collection for the home garden. Emphasis is on good-tasting, easy-to-grow, home garden plants, plus species and cultivars that are interesting and exotic. Landscape qualities are also considered. These ten bananas will form the basic banana grove and garden. Only one cooking banana was included, but gardeners interested in cooking bananas might add one or two from the list "Five Best Cooking Bananas" later in the Appendix.

1  2  3

4  5  6

7  8  9

10  11

### TEN GOOD BANANAS TO GROW

1. *Musa* 'Dwarf Cavendish'

2. *Musa* 'Dwarf Red'

3. *Musa* 'Kru'

4. *Musa* 'Mysore'

5. *Musa* 'Rajapuri'

6. *Musa* 'Ice Cream'

7. *Musa* 'Huamoa'

8. *Musa velutina*

9. *Musella lasiocarpa*

10. *Musa acuminata* ssp. *zebrina*

and one extra:

11. *Musa* 'Super Dwarf Cavendish'

STOKES TROPICALS PUBLISHING CO.

## BEST BANANAS FOR THE LANDSCAPE

This list includes bananas with a range of heights, forms, colors, and foliage. In groups and as specimens they will form a landscape collection. Their edibility was not considered and most are not recommended for an edible grove. These might also be suitable for a large public conservatory/greenhouse. Please check other lists to fit your needs.

1. *Ensete ventricosum*

2. *Ensete maurelii* for bold foliage and plant form.

3. *Musa* 'Rajapuri' because of wind resistance.

4. *Musa* 'Ae Ae' for the variegated foliage—needs a protected site.

5. *Musa acuminata* ssp. *zebrina* for variegated foliage; easier than 'Ae Ae.'

6. *Musa* 'Giant Cavendish' because of its large size and excellent foliage.

7. *Musa* 'Ele Ele,' the Black Hawaiian banana, is large and dramatic.

8. *Musella lasiocarpa*, which has large yellow flowers, hardiness, and a bold plant form.

9. *Musa* 'Super Dwarf Cavendish,' a tropical ground cover.

## SIX TALL BANANAS

Today many commercial export bananas are dwarf or low growing cultivars. These are easier to harvest and cultivate. Since most bananas are grown and consumed locally, height is not a major consideration except for its value in the landscape. Taller bananas are generally more subject to higher winds, drying conditions, and other climatic extremes. By coincidence all of these are edible and include both dessert and cooking types.

1. 25 ft. (7.5 m)
   *Musa* 'Ele Ele'

2. 21 ft. (6.8 m)
   *Musa* 'Saba'

3. 20 ft. (6 m)
   *Musa* 'Orinoco'

4. 20 ft. (6 m)
   *Musa* 'Brazilian'

5. 20 ft. (6 m)
   *Musa* 'Giant Cavendish'

6. 20 ft. (6 m)
   *Musa* 'Monkey Fingers'

## SIX BEST BANANAS FOR CONTAINERS

Bananas in containers have to "earn" the space and extra care. They must offer something more than just good foliage. These have been selected for both very small size and when possible the extra features of attractive inflorescence and interesting fruit. Most of the flowering bananas are suited for cut flower use.

1. *Musa* 'Super Dwarf Cavendish'

2. *Musa mannii*

3. *Musa uranoscopus*

4. *Musella lasiocarpa*

5. *Musa ornata* 'Bronze'

6. *Musa velutina*

# FIVE SMALL BANANAS

Small size is the main consideration. These bananas can be used in the land-scape as a ground cover or in place of a small shrub. Some are suited to con-tainers. The last three "dwarfs" are selected for their small size and excellent fruit production for dessert or cooking uses.

1. 2–3 ft. (.6 to 1 m)
   *Musa mannii*

2. 2–4 ft. (.6 to 1.3 m)
   *Musa* 'Super Dwarf Cavendish'

3. 5 ft. (1.5 m)
   *Musa* 'Dwarf Orinoco'

4. 6 ft. (2 m)
   *Musa* 'Dwarf Cavendish'

5. 7 ft. (2.5 m) *Musa* 'Double Banana' ('Mahoi')

## FIVE BEST DESSERT BANANAS

Taste is, well, "a matter of taste," and each person may detect more flavor or subtlety than the next. Many people rate the following bananas very highly for overall flavor. 'Grand Nain' is the basic good-tasting banana, but the others all offer variations with overtones of acid, apple, ice cream, honey, etc. In addition to these five bananas, the "red bananas" are all popular for eating from the home garden.

1. *Musa* 'Grand Nain'

2. *Musa* 'Ice Cream'

3. *Musa* 'Brazilian'

4. *Musa* 'Mysore'

5. *Musa* 'FHIA-01'

## FIVE BEST COOKING BANANAS

The best bananas for cooking have a starchy texture and mostly bland taste. These are cooked and used as a base for more flavorful additions of sauces and spices. Some have a texture better suited to frying than boiling, and some make excellent "chips." Some recommendations are given in the text. A few will also be sweet when fully ripe and can be eaten raw, but they are never as good as the best dessert types.

1. *Musa* 'Huamoa' (Cooking banana)

2. *Musa* 'Saba' (Cooking banana)

3. *Musa* 'Orinoco' (Cooking banana)

4. *Musa* 'Dwarf Puerto Rican' (Plantain)

5. *Musa* 'African Rhino Horn' (Plantain)

## HARDIEST BANANAS with protection at northern extremes

Banana hardiness is still a highly debated and evolving subject. Until recently many of these had not even been tried outside zones 9 and 10 or warmer. Only a few definite hardiness ratings are given, but many others deserve to be tried—thus the long list of candidates. We suggest that growers in a cold climate try one of the hardy species or cultivars listed, and as you gain experience test others. As more rare high-altitude species come into cultivation, this list could alter drastically. These will always perform better in milder climates. The species and cultivars listed are not likely to flower or fruit in colder climates, but may be grown as herbaceous perennials. During long exposure to freezing temperatures the above ground parts will freeze back. The longer the freezing temperatures persist the greater the 'die back,' with some plants dying down to ground level and returning from the underground frost-free rhizome.

1. *Musa basjoo*—Tried and true through zone 5 with protection, may survive even colder climates.

2. *Musella lasiocarpa*—Still untested, but may be hardy to zone 5 or 6.

3. *Musa velutina*—Hardy to at least zone 7.

   Candidates to try: *Musa* 'Dwarf Cavendish,' Musa 'Orinoco,' *Musa sikkimensis*, Musa 'Rajapuri,' Musa 'Mysore,' and *Ensete glaucum* when available.

1

2

3

## TEN COLLECTORS' BANANAS

The collector seeks odd bananas, rare species, colorful and unusual fruit or foliage, and other characteristics. Some of these are costly to obtain, difficult to grow, and harder still to flower and fruit. The challenge of amassing this collection will be rewarded by a unique cross section of the banana family. Refer to the text for each unique characteristic.

1. *Ensete maurelii*

2. *Musa basjoo*

3. *Musa mannii*

4. *Musella lasiocarpa*

5. *Musa* 'Ae Ae'

6. *Musa balbisiana* 'Burmese Blue Banana'

7. *Musa* 'Ele Ele'

8. *Musa* 'Kru'

9. *Musa* 'Praying Hands'

10. *Musa* 'Red Iholene'

and one extra,

11. *Musa* 'Super Dwarf Cavendish'

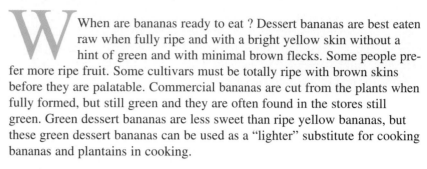

# RECIPES

W When are bananas ready to eat ? Dessert bananas are best eaten raw when fully ripe and with a bright yellow skin without a hint of green and with minimal brown flecks. Some people prefer more ripe fruit. Some cultivars must be totally ripe with brown skins before they are palatable. Commercial bananas are cut from the plants when fully formed, but still green and they are often found in the stores still green. Green dessert bananas are less sweet than ripe yellow bananas, but these green dessert bananas can be used as a "lighter" substitute for cooking bananas and plantains in cooking.

Dessert bananas used in banana bread can be very ripe, even black. The fruit will be very sweet and mushy, but that is acceptable. When you need to keep the shape of the fruit, the banana should not be over ripe.

Even in native banana growing areas, the fruit is often cut green and allowed to ripen off the plant. Many dessert banana cultivars listed in this book may not have exactly the same characters and ripen only when black or ripen when still green or turn red when ripe. *Caveat emptor*: know your bananas.

Plantains and cooking bananas are usually eaten cooked in the green state. If allowed to ripen, they will turn black, but their sturdy flesh will remain firm longer. When ripe they may be sweet enough to eat raw. Plantains and cooking bananas should be cooked until fully tender and not allowed to over-cook or turn to mush. When cooked all bananas increase in sweetness.

Bananas are not just for eating out of hand. They are remarkably flexible as ingredients in everything from soup to main dishes, drinks and desserts. Following are a few less common recipes.

## TOSTONES

This is one of the most widespread and basic recipes for plantains and cooking bananas. Slight variations are found throughout Central and South America, the Caribbean, Asia, and Polynesia. The name "tostones" is derived from Spanish. They are also known as "toastone'" and "patacones."

This is a basic recipe. Feel free to add toppings and to use as a side dish to all kinds of meat and vegetable entrees.

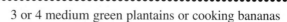

3 or 4 medium green plantains or cooking bananas

Peanut or canola oil as needed for frying

Salt to taste

Bananas are rich in vitamins C and B-6 and potassium.

Bananas are about 75% water.

Peel the fruit by cutting off the top, bottom, and ridges. Then peel or cut off the rest of the skin. This will take some practice.

Slice them diagonally into 1/2- to 1-in. thick slices. The thickness is a matter of taste. We recommend 1/2 in. slices the first time, and then you may alter to suit your own taste.

Pour about 1/2 in. of oil into a heavy pan. When the oil has reached medium-to-high heat, add the slices and brown on one side. Turn over and brown again.

Tostones—refried, flattened green plantains—with onions.

Some people like to mash the slices slightly as they soften and cook, others do not touch them. When browned and crispy to your liking, remove and drain on paper towels.

Salt to taste.

Serve as a side dish with condiments of your choice.

•••

Variations. After peeling the fruit and while the oil is heating, salt the slices and cover in cold water. Drain and fry as above.

After browning and draining, mash the slices to a thinner, wider shape and fry again to make them crispier. The first frying will soften the plantain enough to mash them fairly flat.

•••

Try serving tostones with homemade salsa, pico de gallo, or any pasta sauce such as a tomato-based marinara or Alfredo. They go well as an accompaniment to meat stews with heavy gravies. They can also be served for dessert with maple syrup, berries, and whipped cream. Tostones are a basic food and can be used in a wide variety of ways.

•••

One banana averages 75 calories.

A ripe dessert banana may contain up to 21% sugar.

Bananas have almost no fat.

## BANANA FLOWERS

The immature banana flower is an ingredient in Chinese food and many dishes in Southeast Asia. These can be found in Asian grocery stores all around the world. The greatest difficulty to its use in food is the lack of familiarity in preparing the basic ingredient.

When purchased from the market or picked from the tree, choose a large, firm flower head that will look something like a deep green or red or purple ear of corn still in its shucks.

(Incidentally, northern growers may find a developing inflorescence has been nipped back or killed by frost. It is still possible to salvage a nice banana flower and use it to make a special dish. )

Peel back the outer sheaths (actually bracts protecting the flowers) until the color has become fairly pale and the parts tender—or crisp. One way to speed this up is to cut the flower lengthwise.

The larger female flowers usually with minibananas attached (closest to the cut stem) should be removed. Trim and select only the palest, crunchiest parts of the flower. This will include bracts, male flowers, and some of the main stalk, but the stalk is too tough and fibrous to eat.

Do not be discouraged if only half or less of the entire flower ends up in the pot. This process is to give you a start in hopes you'll gain experience and try other ways.

These pieces and parts should be cut into 1-in. wide or smaller sections and chunks. At this stage the material is inedible. It must be soaked for about half an hour in a salt solution. Add a bit of lemon juice or vinegar to keep the parts from turning dark.

While the flower parts are soaking, break up the layers of bracts to make sure the salt water penetrates deeply to remove the tannins. You may swirl and shake up the pieces during this time. Rinse thoroughly under cold running water to remove the salt and all dissolved components.

I recommend a quick blanching in boiling water to fix the flower parts. Bring a pot of water to boil, then add a teaspoon or so of salt and a teaspoon of lemon juice or vinegar depending on the quantities of banana flowers being treated. When the water is boiling well, dump all the parts into the water. Bring back to a boil and drain. Rinse in cool water. The flower is now ready to use in food or store in the refrigerator for future use.

The taste of the flower parts is rather bland, but they readily absorb other flavors. In Chinese food they can be stir-fried with shredded onions and a touch of a very light soy sauce. Add a drop or two of sesame oil before serving as a

In Uganda and Tanzania, a nutritious beer is brewed from bananas. Although various cultivars can be used, only certain ones are used just for this drink.

simple side dish. In Polynesian cooking they are often cooked with coconut milk and even a bit of curry.

They should retain their pale color and crispy texture. The final treatment, sauce, and accompaniments are open to your imagination.

## BANANA BREAD

In many western countries almost the only use of cooked bananas is the nearly ubiquitous banana bread. There must be hundreds of variations including a host of complementary fruits (apricot/banana, orange/banana, etc.) and lacings with everything from pecans to coconut. The following is a slightly spicy variant that is elegant when spread with cream cheese or served "as is." This recipe is printed by permission from *The Banana Lover's Cookbook* (see "Additional Readings").

LOVE LANE BANANA BREAD

1/2 cup butter, softened to room temperature

1 cup sugar

2 eggs

*zeste* and juice of 1 orange

4 ripe bananas

2 cups all-purpose flour

1 teaspoon baking soda

1/2 teaspoon salt

1/2 teaspoon nutmeg

1/4 teaspoon ground ginger

•••

**Variation:** Add one of the following: 1 cup coarsely chopped walnuts, black walnuts, peanuts, pecans, finely chopped dates, golden raisins, or shredded coconut.

The Guinness Book of World Records lists the world's largest banana split as being 1-mile 99-yards long and containing 11,333 bananas—split, of course.

Preheat oven to 350°F. Grease and flour a 9 x 5 in. loaf pan.

In a large mixing bowl and using an electric mixer, cream butter and sugar together. Add eggs and beat until fluffy. Add orange *zeste*, juice, and bananas, beating to combine.

Add remaining dry ingredients and beat just enough to incorporate completely.

Pour into prepared pan and bake for 1 hour or until wooden toothpick inserted in center of pan comes out clean. Remove pan from oven and allow to cool in the pan for 10 minutes. Invert onto wire rack to complete cooling.

Yield 1 loaf.

**Main Dish**

Bananas are staple foods in many countries and used in a wide variety of dishes with meat, chicken, and fish as a main meal. They are little used in American and European cooking, so try using them as a substitute for potatoes or even squash. For those unfamiliar with using these "exotic" ingredients, here's a simple substitution.

## STEW

**Banana "Stew"**—Use any stew recipe that includes beef, pork, or chicken, a variety of vegetables, and requires at least 1 hour of cooking. Prepare the stew as usual, cooking meats and vegetables according to your usual recipe. About 30–40 minutes before cooking is complete, peel 2 or 3 medium-sized fruit and cut into 1 or 2 in. lengths. Add to cooking stew and continue to cook until tender.

You may also use green bananas from a supermarket and follow these directions except cook for 15–20 minutes. Green bananas give a less starchy taste and added sweetness when cooked.

Bananas are especially good combined with chicken or pork.

Pictured above is a Cuban meal featuring banana chips (Mariquitas) with guacamole.. To the right is a typical Cuban dish—picadillo habanero with maduros (fried ripe, sweet plantains).

# USDA HARDINESS ZONE MAP

See page 104 for detailed explanation.

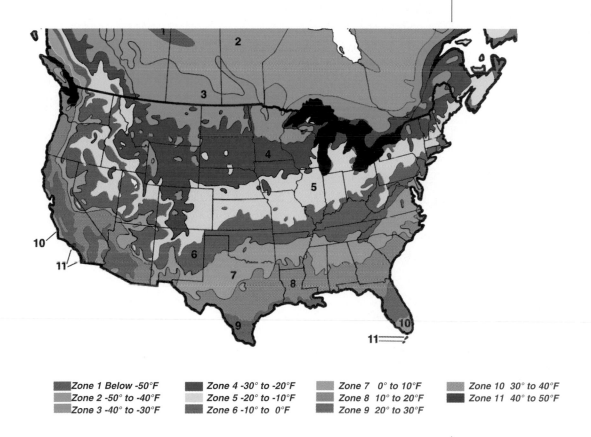

| | | | | |
|---|---|---|---|---|
| Zone 1 Below -50°F | Zone 4 -30° to -20°F | Zone 7  0° to 10°F | Zone 10  30° to 40°F |
| Zone 2 -50° to -40°F | Zone 5 -20° to -10°F | Zone 8  10° to 20°F | Zone 11  40° to 50°F |
| Zone 3 -40° to -30°F | Zone 6 -10° to  0°F | Zone 9  20° to 30°F | |

## WHERE TO BUY BANANAS: SOURCES

Bananas can be shipped in many different forms from seeds to rhizomes or growing plants. Field-grown plants are often exposed to pathogens, pests, and other problems. Many garden bananas are now produced through tissue culture to cut down on these problems. Buyer beware: ask and give preference for certified disease- and pest-free plants.

**Aloha Tropicals**

1247 Browning Ct.

Vista, CA 92083

Phone:   (760) 941-0920

Fax:      (760) 941-0920

Website: www.alohatropicals.com

E-mail:  alohatrop@aol.com

Current website lists five ornamental bananas and over 20 fruiting cultivars, but expect this to change and expand, even double. They specialize in exotic tropicals of all sorts with extensive *Heliconia* offerings. They sell locally and internationally, through mail order and via the website.

**J. D. Andersen Nursery**

2790  Marvinga Lane

Fallbrook, CA 92028

Phone:   (949) 361-3652

Fax:      (949) 492-2198

Website: www.pe.net/~maxson/jdander.htm

E-mail:  jdapalms@earthlink.net

The website lists more than 50 cultivars, but look for more soon. Jerry Andersen thinks that the variety 'Manzan' is best for growing in southern California. Their plants are field grown. The nine-acre nursery is open by appointment only; please call first. They sell locally and by mail order in the U.S. and internationally. Price list is $2 or free at the website.

**Going Bananas**

24401 SW 197 Ave

Homestead FL 33031

Phone:   (305) 247-0397

Fax:      (305) 247-7877

Website: www.zoneten.com/goingbananas.htm

E-mail:  goingbananas@bellsouth.net

This is a specialty-source nursery for bananas with many different cultivars available. Don and Katie Chafin specialize in home-style service, information, and education. They sell by mail order locally and internationally. They will help new growers to get the plants best suited to their climates.

## Stokes Tropicals

P.O. Box 9868

New Iberia LA 70562-9868

Phone:   1-800-624-9706

Fax:      (337) 365-6991

Website: www.stokestropicals.com

E-mail:  info@stokestropicals.com

Stokes Tropicals carries nearly all current cultivars of bananas plus a large variety of other tropical plants. New banana cultivars and species are continuously sought out, tested, and propagated for commercial release. They sell locally, via mail order and through their website, which often boasts special deals. Color pictures of all bananas are available on the website. Nearly all bananas are tissue cultured and all are guaranteed pathogen and pest free. Although a large nursery, Glenn Stokes and his friendly staff emphasize personal service. International shipping is also available on inquiry. The full-color tropical plant guide and catalog with good photos and descriptions costs $7.95, but is refundable on the first order.

## The Banana Tree Inc.

715 Northampton St.

Easton, PA 18042

Phone:   (610) 253-9589

Fax:      (610) 253-4864

Website: www.banana-tree.com

The Banana Tree sells exclusively through their website. They offer a few cultivars of banana plants and a half dozen or so more species by seed. Selection varies, so they suggest you check the site as new items appear regularly. They ship in the U.S. and internationally. They also have an extensive selection of *Heliconia* and unusual tropical plants.

## The Rare Palm Seed Site

Rare Palm and Banana Seeds

Martin Gibbons & Tobias W. Spanner

c/o The Palm Centre

Ham Central Nursery

Ham St., Ham

Richmond, Surrey

TW10 7HA United Kingdom

Phone:   ++44 181 255 6191

Fax:      ++44 181 255 6192

Website: www.rarepalmseed.com/

E-Mail:  mail@rarepalmseeds.com

*(Continued)*

Although this website business is a wholesale seed source targeted at nursery growers, it has one of the best lists of banana seeds, including rare species, only available on an irregular basis, such as *Musa sikkimensis*, *Ensete superbum*, and other collector's items. Seeds are sold by the hundreds and thousands and more.*

They also operate nurseries in both England and Germany that sell plants locally, and catalogs are available by mail, fax, e-mail, or on the web at www.palmcentre.co.uk or www.palmeperpaket.de

*\*Small packets of 10 seeds are now available for most varieties.*

Upper left: the bloom of a *Musa ornata* hybrid; upper right: a *Musa* 'Dwarf Thai' banana; lower left the bloom of *Musa* 'Pelipita', and lower right shows the fruit of a *Musa* 'Iqcpog.'

# WHERE TO SEE BANANAS: Public Gardens

**Balboa Park**
1549 El Prado San Diego, CA 92101, USA

**Fairchild Tropical Garden**
10901 Old Cutler Road, Coral Gables (Miami), FL 33156, USA

**Marie Selby Botanical Gardens**
811 Palm Avenue, Sarasota, FL 34236, USA

**Kebun Raya**
Bogor, Java, Indonesia

**Harold L. Lyon Arboretum**
University of Hawaii at Manoa, 3860 Manoa Road, Honolulu, HI 96822, USA

**Peradeniya Botanical Garden**
Kandy, Sri Lanka

**Royal Botanic Gardens**
Kew, Surrey, TW9 3AB, UK

**Quail Botanical Gardens**
230 Quail Gardens Drive, Encinitas, CA 92023, USA

**Singapore Botanic Garden**
Singapore

**Siwali Garden**
Grand Palace, Bangkok, Thailand

## ADDITIONAL READINGS

Abella, A. *The Total Banana*. New York: Harcourt Brace Jovanovich,1979.

Chamber, C., ed. "Year of the Banana" special issue. *California Rare Fruit Growers*. Vol. 20: 1988.

Constantine, D. "The Musaceae." www.users.globalnet.co.uk/~drc/

Jenkins, V. S. *Bananas: An American History* Smithsonian Institution Press. Washington, D.C., 2000

Lessard, W. O. *The Complete Book of Bananas*.  Self-published, 1992.

Lindquist, C. *The Banana Lover's Cookbook*. New York: St. Martin's Press, 1993.

Robinson, J. C. *Bananas and Plantains*. Oxon, U.K.: CAB International, 1996.

Simmonds, N. W. *Bananas* (2nd edition). Essex, U.K.: Longman Group Limited, 1966.

Stokes, G. M. *Bananas.* Over the Hedge, Vol. 4, no. 6 (Nov./Dec. 1998): 50–56, 62.

Stokes, G. M. *Tropical Plant Guide/Catalog*. Stokes Tropicals Publishing Co., New Iberia, LA., 2000.

Wolverton, B. C. *How to Grow Fresh Air: Fifty Houseplants that Purify Your Home or Office*. New York: Penguin Books, 1997.

# INDEX